LIFE ISSUES

EMOTIONAL DISORDERS

by Dr. M. Nikki Goldman

Marshall Cavendish
NEW YORK • LONDON • TORONTO • SYDNEY

Published by Marshall Cavendish Corporation
2415 Jerusalem Avenue
North Bellmore, New York 11710
USA

Library of Congress Cataloging-in-Publication Data

Goldman, M. Nikki,
    Emotional disorders / M. Nikki Goldman.
      p.   cm. — (Life issues)
    Includes bibliographical references and index.
    ISBN 1-85435-687-9 (set.) — ISBN 1-85435-619-4 :
    1. Depression, Mental—Juvenile literature. 2. Anxiety—Juvenile
literature. 3. Eating disorders—Juvenile literature. 4. Substance
abuse—Juvenile literature. 5. Schizophrenia—Juvenile literature.
[1. Mental illness.] I. Title. II. Series.
RC454.G589 1994
616.85'27—dc20   93-42609
                                    CIP
                                    AC

Produced by The Creative Spark
Editor: Gregory Lee
Art direction: Robert Court
Design: Mary Francis-DeMarois, Robert Court
Page layout, graphic illustration: Mary Francis-DeMarois

Marshall Cavendish editorial director: Evelyn M. Fazio
Marshall Cavendish editorial consultant: Marylee Knowlton
Marshall Cavendish production manager: Ruth Toda

Printed and bound in the United States of America

Photographic Note
Several persons depicted in this book are photographic models; their appearance in these photographs is solely to
dramatize some of the situations and choices facing readers of the Life Issues series.

Photo Credits
Christie Costanzo: 88
The Image Works: 32 (M. Bernsau); 44 (T. Michaels); 52 (Harriet Gans); 60 (Mel Rosenthal); 69 (M. Antman);
    81 (Michael Siluk)
Impact Visuals: 76 (Dan Habib)
PhotoEdit: 6 (Richard Hutchings); 8, 17, 39, 71 (Tony Freeman); 12 (Cleo Freelance Photo); 18, 54 (Alan Oddie);
    30, 37, 49 (David Young-Wolf); 62, 74, 79 (Mary Kate Denny); 64 (Robert Brenner); 85 (Michael Newman)
Photo Researchers, Inc.: 23 (J. Gerard Smith); 42 (Susan Rosenburg); 48 (Rapho)
Photo Researchers, Inc./Science Photo Library: 4 (Paul Fletcher); 10, 28 (Oscar Burriel/Latin Stock);
    21 (Philippe Plailly); 25 (Louise Williams)

Cover photo PhotoEdit (Paul Conklin)

Acknowledgments
The publisher would like to thank Myra Alfreds, C.S.W., Program Director for Children's Mental Health
Services, Westchester County Department of Community Mental Health, for reviewing this manuscript.

TABLE OF CONTENTS

PROLOGUE

When you break a bone or catch a cold, you visit the doctor. The physician provides you with a remedy to help you recover. When you know what the problem is and take action, you feel in control of your life. You can focus all your attention on getting well. What do you do when you have an emotional disorder, however, and not a physical problem?

Millions of people in the United States are afflicted with emotional disorders. Their families and friends often suffer with them. This book reviews some of the events and situations that cause people to develop these difficulties. The purpose of this book is to provide clear information about various disorders and the variety of options available to help you or someone you know cope with them.

The words "emotional disorders" probably bring to mind some stereotypes. You may have seen someone sitting at a bus stop talking out loud to an imaginary person or shouting a sermon to no one in particular. While these are clearly behaviors of individuals who suffer from severe emotional problems, there are many people whose illnesses are not so obvious: Teens who rely on drugs to get them through the day; parents who sit listlessly in front of the television day after day, barely functioning; the young girl whose concern about her appearance is so severe it causes her to lose a dangerous amount of weight. All of these are types of emotional disorders.

One aim of this book is to show that normal-looking, everyday people also suffer from debilitating problems. Those who endure this silent pain can be a family member, a best friend, or your own parents. Many people who do their best to live their lives and appear normal on the outside experience tremendous emotional hurt inside. Learning to feel empathy for others is crucial to helping them recover from emotional problems. Understanding emotional disorders and not judging the people who suffer from them is the key to helping us all become healthy, happy, and productive individuals.

1

Depression, Anxiety Disorders, and Schizophrenia

I didn't feel very good. I felt like my illness was my fault.
I was kind of sad. I just walked around wanting to be alone.
I didn't have any friends.
—Seth, age 14, recalling his depression

When Alicia heard her boyfriend's family was moving to another state, she was upset. This was something she could not control and she knew it. She'd have to learn to live with it. Her feelings swelled up within her and she knew she'd have to find an outlet for her frustration. Gymnastics and dance were her favorite things to do as a release when she was upset. After she got the bad news, she went to the school gym and practiced her dance routine. She put every ounce of energy she had into it. She danced for hours. By the time she was through, she was exhausted. She sat down on the floor dripping with perspiration from her hard workout. Her mind began to wander back to the unhappy situation. This time, however, when she thought about it, something was different. She started to have some happy thoughts about it. She realized her boyfriend would be living in the very next state. She could visit him at least once a month on a weekend. She could apply to three colleges that would put her within an hour's drive of his new home. College was only a year away, so it wouldn't be long until they could be together again.

When times are tough and life is upsetting, having a good workout or doing your favorite activity can help clear your mind and help you see things from a better perspective.

Being stuck in traffic, having your favorite TV show cancelled—these are events we have little or no control over. Being able to accept calmly such frustrations or disappointments is a sign of mental health.

Suddenly she felt better. Although she couldn't do anything about her boyfriend's circumstances, she realized she could do something about her own.

Kevin wanted to take drivers' education so he could get his license at age 16 instead of waiting until he was 17. His parents would not let him take the class. His grades were below average and they felt the additional responsibility would distract him from his studies. Kevin felt angry and extremely frustrated. He wanted to change his parents' decision so he could have what he wanted. At first, he argued with them. This didn't work and he was left with feelings of helplessness. He couldn't change these circumstances and he wasn't willing to accept them. His feelings were getting the better of him. He felt like a volcano ready to explode. He knew he needed to do something, but he didn't know what. When his parents were asleep, he took the keys to the car and went for a drive. Ten minutes later, he crashed into another car and was seriously injured.

The key to mental health is in our ability to adapt to changing circumstances. In life, there are always situations that occur that are beyond our control. You may make plans to see your favorite football team play. On the day of the game, there's a snow storm and the event is canceled. A normal reaction is to be disappointed. You might throw a ball against a wall for a half-hour to let out some of the frustration. After a while, however, you begin to bounce back and move on to other things. You realize you'll get to see the game when it is rescheduled and the loss is only temporary. This shows an ability to be flexible.

To people who are emotionally unbalanced, however, this same situation might cause so much stress and disappointment that they are unable to resume their normal activity. They might, for example, brood for a long period of time. They might become so unhappy they take it out on a younger brother or sister by picking a fight. They can even cross the line into criminal behavior, such as stealing a car to go for a joy ride to release their aggression. Perhaps they'll indulge in some drugs in order to make themselves feel better. These are all overreactions to a normal situation.

Whether the person brooded or bounced the ball, a reaction took place in order to cope with disappointment. The reaction expressed itself in both behavior and mood or feeling. First, it was the amount of intensity that made the difference between a healthy response and an unhealthy one. There was also a thought process that accompanied the feeling. For example, in the first instance, the person was probably thinking, "I wish I knew this was going to happen. I'd have made other plans. Instead, I'm stuck here with nothing to do." Then, after a short while, the thoughts refocused.

Second, the choice about how to behave or act on the feelings also determines emotional fitness and balance. When people are emotionally disordered or unbalanced, they don't use their ability to make choices. They tend to react automatically to situations without thinking them through. They fall prey to being a victim and are unaware of their sense of personal power. When a reaction to life circumstances becomes extreme, emotional disorders can develop.

EMOTIONAL DISORDERS

Emotional disorders can appear in many different forms. They can affect people's moods so severely that sufferers cannot even get out of bed. These disorders can create such anxiety that individuals may not be able to sleep at night. In all cases, these disorders affect the ability to carry out normal day-to-day activity to various degrees. Psychologists have put these illnesses into categories and given them names. The purpose of this is to help identify the problems people may have. Therapists can then determine which treatment would be best for their patients.

Affective disorders or mood disorders. Two examples of mood disorders are bipolar disorder (previously called manic depression) and depression. These affect people's moods in the extreme. Sometimes people feel very low and unhappy. In other instances, they feel so happy and excited that they are out of control.

Anxiety disorders. These include phobias and Post Traumatic Stress Disorder (PTSD). Fears become overwhelming.

Eating disorders. This category has only recently been added and includes bulimia, anorexia, and compulsive eating. Food gets used like a drug. People's body images become extremely distorted.

Schizophrenia. This chemical disorder affects people's ability to perceive reality.

Substance and alcohol abuse. With these disorders, people misuse drugs and alcohol to help cope with life.

Severe emotional disorders such as depression and schizophrenia reduce or completely block the ability to think rationally and stay in control of our daily lives.

AFFECTIVE DISORDERS

Everyone feels depressed at one time or another, but sometimes the depression becomes very serious and needs treatment. Just what is the difference between normal unhappiness and the kind of sadness that can be damaging to a person? Let's take a look at three people who experience these feelings.

Seth became ill with a severe case of chicken pox. As a result, he suffered an unusual side effect. Many of the muscles in his face were paralyzed. He couldn't smile at all. When he talked, his upper lip was stiff. This made his speech sound strange and stilted. It was often difficult to understand his words. Kids at school teased him. This depressed him so much that he didn't want to be around others, and it showed. Other kids didn't want to be around him either. This created a vicious cycle of loneliness.

"My parents helped me out a lot," Seth remembers. "They talked to me and made me feel better. They told me it doesn't matter what anyone else thinks. It only matters what I think. Then my self-esteem went up and I didn't really care that the kids were calling me names." Seth's depression was a normal reaction to a loss in his life—the loss of his health. He was able to cope with his negative experience by using his parents as a source of support and his own ability to adapt his thinking. Seth's type of depression is a typical occurrence in everyday life.

Jim's dad was often away on business. When he was home, he was so preoccupied with his work that he paid very little attention to Jim. Doing well in school didn't capture his notice. Neither did doing poorly. Sports produced the same result: No reaction. If Jim came home with a trophy, his dad gave a perfunctory nod of his head and a barely audible, "Very nice, son." Then he went back to his work. Even when Jim got kicked off the team, his dad didn't have enough time to acknowledge his son's unhappy feelings. After awhile, Jim began to lose interest in life. He tossed and turned at night, unable to sleep. He felt lonely and didn't have energy to pursue his friendships. He rarely had much of an appetite and was losing weight. These feelings continued for about a year until Jim began to have thoughts of suicide. Jim was suffering from major depression.

Julie never quite felt happy. Although she could become somewhat involved in an activity for a short period of time, when the activity was over, she went back to her usual mood. She experienced boredom a great deal of the time. Julie suffered from mild chronic depression.

CAUSES OF DEPRESSION

Parental pressure can be one cause of depression among teens. Although young people are at the age when they are seeking more independence, it is still natural to want to fulfill their parents' expectations. For example, Julie tried to be the perfect child. It seemed like no matter what she did, however, she could not meet her parents' standards. "My parents are always on my case about one thing or another. If I get a 'B' on a test, they ask why I didn't get an 'A.' If I get an 'A,' they ask why I didn't feed the dog on time. It seems like I can never win." The harder she tried, the more they asked of her.

School can be stressful. Some young people experience severe mood disorders such as depression because of academic pressures.

Pressures from school are another cause of depression. Competition between students creates a great deal of tension. A girl might get average grades, yet she sees her peers getting rewards for excelling. They may be acknowledged by being put on the honor role or getting more attention from teachers or others. She may feel she is worthless unless she can shine like the other students. If she is really performing at her full capacity, however, the frustration from being unable to improve may deepen.

Loneliness is a common source of depression. All human beings need acceptance, support, and companionship. Teens are particularly susceptible to this need to be liked. Finding one's niche or group where one feels comfortable is not always easy. Sometimes, loneliness is due to loss. Many parents are divorced. An adolescent may not see one or the other parent as often as she used to when they were together. Even when both parents live nearby and spend as much time with their child as before, there may be a feeling of missing the family unit as it once was.

Feelings of loss can come from many other things as well. They can be from the loss of a loved one due to death or any form of separation. Moving to a new neighborhood or new school can trigger feelings of emptiness. A serious illness in a member of the family, or one's own, may cause these emotions, too.

Feeling alone can stem from feeling misunderstood; the person feels he or she is the only one who experiences something. "I feel like there is something wrong with me," said Julie. "I see other kids having fun, but I never seem to enjoy myself." Julie sees herself as the only one with the problem. Her perception blocks out part of the picture. She is only able to see herself as different from others. If she expressed her feelings to others, she would see that many share her discontent.

RECOGNIZING DEPRESSION

Several symptoms indicate a depression is present. Learning to recognize these can assist in realizing help is needed. The most common symptoms of depression are:

- Feelings of self-hatred and worthlessness
- Sleeping problems
- Exhaustion without obvious cause
- Lack of interest in friends
- Poor performance at school or work
- Loss of appetite, or an increase in appetite to the point of overeating
- Irritability and restless behavior

RECOGNIZING DEPRESSION

The symptoms of depression can fit into four general categories: behavioral patterns, moods or feelings, thinking patterns, and physical symptoms.

The test below can help determine if you're suffering from depression. Respond to each description by recording how true it is for you. For example, next to "Crying spells," check the column that reflects how often you have them (Almost Always, Often, Rarely, or Never). If you check two or more items from each section with an Often or Almost Always, you may be suffering from some form of depression. Note: This test should be used only as an indicator that something may be amiss. You should not try to diagnose yourself. If you believe you're depressed, seek someone else's help and learn more about it.

1. BEHAVIORAL PATTERNS

	Almost Always	Often	Rarely	Never
Crying spells (with no apparent cause)	❑	❑	❑	❑
Withdrawal from family	❑	❑	❑	❑
Withdrawal from friends	❑	❑	❑	❑
Withdrawal from situations/ events you previously enjoyed	❑	❑	❑	❑
Clothes and body unwashed	❑	❑	❑	❑
Bedroom sloppy and disorganized	❑	❑	❑	❑
Loss of appetite or dramatic increase in appetite	❑	❑	❑	❑
Active with several sex partners within a short period of time	❑	❑	❑	❑
Feeling frustrated without apparent cause	❑	❑	❑	❑

2. MOOD or FEELINGS

	Almost Always	Often	Rarely	Never
Radical mood swings (from very low to overly excited)	❑	❑	❑	❑
Irritated easily	❑	❑	❑	❑
Feeling down, as if there's a cloud hanging over your head	❑	❑	❑	❑
Feeling afraid or timid	❑	❑	❑	❑
Feeling like everything is too much effort	❑	❑	❑	❑

3. THINKING PATTERNS

	Almost Always	Often	Rarely	Never
Difficulty concentrating due to distracting thoughts	❏	❏	❏	❏
Hyper thinking; going rapidly from one thought to the next	❏	❏	❏	❏

Negative thoughts such as:

	Almost Always	Often	Rarely	Never
I wish I were better looking	❏	❏	❏	❏
I can't do anything right	❏	❏	❏	❏
People don't like me	❏	❏	❏	❏
I hate the way I look	❏	❏	❏	❏
Things will never change	❏	❏	❏	❏
No one would care if I died	❏	❏	❏	❏
I hate my life	❏	❏	❏	❏
I feel stupid	❏	❏	❏	❏

4. PHYSICAL SYMPTOMS

	Almost Always	Often	Rarely	Never
Digestive problems	❏	❏	❏	❏
Muscle aches and pains	❏	❏	❏	❏
Not feeling well	❏	❏	❏	❏
Body feels heavy	❏	❏	❏	❏
Flatness or drawn feeling in facial muscles	❏	❏	❏	❏

Source: Adapted from "Depression: How to Recognize It, Cure It, and Grow from It," by Wina Sturgeon.

BIPOLAR DISORDER

I magine you are on a roller coaster. You are no longer having fun, yet you are locked in and can't get off. This trapped feeling changes a ride that was once exciting and joyful into a journey of torment and agony. This analogy represents the emotional roller coaster of one who suffers from bipolar disorder.

Robyn was energized. This was the first time in her life she felt such excitement. She was overly happy. Along with this enthusiasm was a feeling of constant agitation. She took on several new and dangerous hobbies. Bungee jumping was one of her new thrills. She never gave a thought to the possible dangers. She participated in many activities in the morning before school, then went through a full day of classes participating in each one with an exaggerated enthusiasm. She felt high and euphoric. She talked vivaciously during class discussions and was full of new and imaginative ideas. Her thoughts came to her rapidly, one after the other, without giving her a moment in between. As she walked from one classroom to the other, she sought out friends with whom to chat endlessly. When she didn't see anyone she knew, she'd turn to the person walking next to her and make conversation anyway. Her speech was very rapid and non-stop. No one could get in a word.

People were drawn to Robyn's incredible energy and magnetism. Her self-esteem was inflated. She thought she was a genius and believed she would one day be discovered and made famous for her talents. One day, she took her parents' credit cards and charged thousands of dollars worth of clothes. She bought her friends outfits. She even gave money away to strangers. This level of hyperactivity continued for five days. She had so much energy, she didn't seem to need any sleep. After this episode, she fell into a profound depression. She couldn't get out of bed. She slept for days and lost all interest in life. She felt guilty and ashamed of all the things she'd been doing. Her parents recognized that something was wrong, so they took her to a psychiatrist. Robyn was diagnosed as having bipolar disorder.

This emotional disturbance is characterized by its broad swing of moods. These swings differ from normal mood changes. They are usually sustained over long periods of time, lasting days, weeks, or even months. An individual who suffers from this is likely to feel ecstatic during the high times, and so depressed she can't get out of bed during the low stages. The high periods are so extreme she may not sleep for days. The individual feels energized and happy and loves the intensity of the experience. She may behave in bizarre ways, such as spending money or taking trips to far-away places on sheer impulse, only to regret it after she has come down from her manic episode. The depression is equally as profound, with symptoms that include a lack of energy and loss of concentration. The person is now debilitated by the low side of the disease.

The onset of bipolar disorder generally occurs between adolescence and early adulthood. The typical treatment includes medication to stabilize the mood swings and private and/or group therapy. Group support can help with the feelings of shame regarding the out-of-control behavior. Tests of those who suffer from this disorder reveal a chemical imbalance in the brain. This imbalance is not their fault; it is a sickness, just like cancer or any other physical ailment.

ANXIETY AND ANXIETY DISORDERS

J oan refused to go to school. The truant officer either called her or showed up at her home on a regular basis. She hated being in an environment where there were lots of people. She felt a terrible feeling of dread and anxiety in public places. She spent most of her time by herself watching television. She didn't have many friends. On the occasions when she would go to see them, however, she would become very uncomfortable and leave after a short time. She avoided many situations where there were people, particularly large groups of people.

One time, she managed to get herself to go to the park and ride her bicycle with her friends. She suddenly became very aware of the other youngsters playing nearby and began to have negative

People who suffer episodes of anxiety can experience them anywhere at anytime, for no apparent reason.

thoughts about herself: "I wonder what they think of what I'm doing. Maybe they think I look foolish." Joan knew they weren't thinking anything about her at all. She could see they were busy playing their own games, but she couldn't help "feeling" as if they were looking at her. She experienced an extreme form of self-consciousness. She became so tense, she decided to go home. In fact, her fear was so profound, she was struck by a feeling of being paralyzed. She tried to get herself to go home for what felt like forever. All she could do was sit there and think about how much she wanted to be in the safety of her own house, but she couldn't move.

Her thoughts continued to spin in her head like a bicycle wheel stuck in the mud: No matter how hard one tries to pedal, the wheel just spins. These feelings are the reason Joan rarely ventured out. Joan has a social phobia as well as agoraphobia. After awhile, however, she was able to push herself through her fear and anxiety. Getting herself home took a long time and a lot of courage. She talked herself into walking to the nearest tree, telling herself it was only ten feet away and she could make it that short distance. She promised herself she didn't have to go any farther than that; she could sit down under the tree. Once she went that short distance, it took another 20 minutes to talk herself into going another few feet. She did this all the way home.

Ted is the football captain. He is successful in school, has many friends, and is generally content with his life. One day, however, he is stuck in the corner of the locker room frozen with fear. His heart is pounding and his forehead is covered with perspiration. A spider is using this area for its home. Although Ted knows the spider will not hurt him, it does not lessen his terror. Ted's fear is known as a simple phobia.

A phobia is an overreaction to some event or thing, causing an almost uncontrollable fear in the sufferer. For example, some people are afraid of heights or insects.

PHOBIAS

There are three types of phobias: simple phobia, social phobia, and agoraphobia. A phobia is an intense fear. A normal fear is an emotional and physical reaction to something threatening. A phobia is a similar reaction, but the fear is a reaction to something that is not normally dangerous. The reaction is more intense and out of proportion. In Ted's case, his reaction to the spider is greater than the situation requires. His pounding heart and perspiration are physical signs of his anxiety. Other physical reactions can include heart palpitations, trembling, a feeling of warmth, a dry mouth, sweating, and breathlessness.

Phobias have four outstanding characteristics:

1. The person has an unreasonable physical and emotional reaction to something that is not normally dangerous.
2. The fear persists for a long time and is extremely intense.
3. The fear is so powerful that the person feels he or she cannot control it.
4. The person who suffers avoids the object or situation that is feared.

Agoraphobia is a Greek word meaning "fear of the marketplace" or "place of assembly." Agoraphobics are not actually afraid of the places themselves. They are afraid of their own feelings of fear and anxiety at gatherings.

Joan decided to seek out the help of a therapist to overcome her tremendous anxiety. "I just like being left alone. I don't care about the things other people care about," she said to her therapist.

"Feeling like you just don't care is a defense mechanism," replied her therapist. "You pretend you don't care so you won't have to experience the anxiety you feel in these situations."

"I'm aware of the anxiety I feel," Joan said defensively. "I know when I'm out with other kids, I feel like I want to curl up and hide away."

"So now that you can talk about the anxiety, maybe we can do something about it," said her therapist.

This discussion reveals why Joan wants to avoid situations where there are other people: Her fears are so severe, they affect her ability to function normally. She feels emotionally safe only when she is in the protective environment of her own home. She is not concerned about the dangers that are found in neighborhoods with gangs or other criminals. An irrational fear of her own anxious feelings prevents her from feeling safe. It is difficult for her to adapt.

Some people who suffer from this disorder are debilitated to such an extent that they always stay at home. They are called housebound agoraphobics. In other words, their fear is so extreme and applied to so many situations that they will not leave their home for any reason. They ask others to take care of their errands, such as grocery shopping. Others have the illness, but can carry out some tasks. They may be able to go to school or work, but need to return home immediately afterward. These people are called functional agoraphobics.

Agoraphobics usually have fears and anxiety in more than one situation. Places they fear the most are usually characterized by large crowds, or areas in which there are large spaces. The open spaces can include indoor areas, such as the lobbies of large buildings or assembly halls, and outdoor areas, such as courtyards or meadows. The sufferers know there is no real danger, but continue to feel the fear. In fact, it is not the place or situation they fear. They are afraid of their own feelings of fear. They are worried they might experience these anxious and paralyzing feelings while in public.

Joan felt so immobilized when out at the park, she was afraid she wouldn't be able to make it home. This reinforced her desire to stay home. Each time she thought of going somewhere, she recalled how she felt the last time, so even her memories of fear were confining her.

When people feel anxious before encountering a given situation, it is called negative anticipation. The anticipation of the negative reaction is often worse than the actual event. This explains why agoraphobics spend a great deal of time in a troubled state of mind. Agoraphobics are also subject to depression.

When people spend much of their time worried and concerned about things they cannot control, it is likely to have a depressing effect. Some experts believe agoraphobia is actually a form of depression.

A social phobia is a fear of being criticized, judged, or looked at. The underlying fear is of being embarrassed or ridiculed. Those who suffer from this are usually able to function in other areas of their lives. They simply avoid the one or two situations that cause the anxiety. Some common social phobias include: Fear of public speaking, using public lavatories, eating in public, vomiting, being watched at work, blushing, or being touched. Joan's social fear arose when she played. She was afraid others would think she was foolish. Another girl had a social phobia that kept her from listening to music in her apartment. She was afraid a passerby would hear it and make a negative judgment about the type of music she liked.

Fear of crowds can be a social phobia as well, but it is not the same as agoraphobia. The social fear of crowds is that of being watched. Those with agoraphobia have a fear of feeling enclosed or suffocated by people. Those with the social phobia can avoid the situation and function well in all other areas of their lives. Those with agoraphobia are severely restricted.

Simple phobias are the least damaging. The fear is of a single object or situation, such as Ted's fear of spiders. Some other simple phobias include the fear of snakes, heights, water, dogs, hair, animals, germs, horses, doctors, dentists, flying, intravenous injections, and blood. In most cases, the object of fear can be avoided and the sufferer can lead a normal life. If it spills over into other areas of life, however, it can create a more devastating effect.

Shelly was afraid of having blood taken. Although healthy people don't need blood drawn very often, Shelly's fear prevented her from doing many other normal things. Her fear was so intense, she became very protective of the insides of her elbows (where blood is usually drawn). She kept her arms curved at all times so "no one could come near them" as she described it. She couldn't relax in any situation because her mind was always focused on protecting her arms.

This was even true when her boyfriend kissed her. In fact, the fear of having blood drawn was so extreme, it had even transferred to the arches of her feet. She had an irrational fear that if a doctor or nurse couldn't get to her arms, they would take the blood from her feet. She wouldn't let anyone else near them as well. She refused to go to shoe stores where a shoe salesperson was likely to put the shoe on her.

What prompted her to seek therapy was her desire to get married. She knew a blood test would be required. She also wanted to have children. Pregnancy would no doubt mean confronting her phobia. Fortunately, she sought the help of a hypnotherapist and was able to overcome the problem in a short time.

Hypnosis is one method of psychotherapy. Individuals learn to relax, visualize both uncomfortable thoughts and solutions, and regain control over their fears.

GETTING HELP

Traditional psychotherapy, while successful with many disorders, is not helpful in the area of phobias. Psychotherapy involves talking about the problem, developing insight, and realizing there are many choices about how to handle the problem. Because phobias are irrational, however, talking to another person logically to help them understand that it is "only" a fear falls short of accomplishing the goal. Even the person with the fear knows how unreasonable it is. A change needs to take place below the surface. These fears are lodged in the subconscious mind. Only with the aid of hypnotherapy, visualization, or some other form of therapy that reaches these deeper subconscious areas, can these illogical fears be removed. The appendix of the book has a list of sources for finding hypnotherapists.

SCHOOL PHOBIA

T he name of this disorder is misleading. Children or teenagers with school phobia are not actually afraid of the school itself. They experience fears and anxiety within themselves when they attend school. This anxiety is similar to agoraphobics' fear in that they are each afraid of their own feelings in specific situations. The fear occurs when they must leave the safety and security of their homes and those to whom they are emotionally attached. They then must enter into a world where they are expected to use a wide range of social, emotional, and intellectual skills. Their separation from the people with whom they have the most significant bond is a terrible threat. In fact, experts have come to understand this as a separation anxiety and so renamed the disorder as such.

Those who suffer from separation anxiety may be plagued with thoughts about harm that could come to either themselves or the people to whom they are emotionally attached. This anxiety may express itself in nightmares as well. Their preoccupation with morbid ideas may include those in which they imagine dying or in which their loved ones will die. They may have some sleep disturbances. They fear separation to such an extent that they may need the person to whom they are attached to stay with them until they are asleep.

Their fear of going to school may not be something in their awareness. Instead, they may feel sick with stomach aches, headaches or vomiting, etc., when it is time to go to school, yet feel fine when school is over. This does not mean they are lying or deliberately trying to get away with something by pretending they are sick. Their tension and stress create feelings in their bodies as if they are actually sick. Some who suffer from this disorder will deny their attachment to the mother or father or whomever else, but their behavior will reveal their true emotions. They will tend to cling to the people to whom they feel close.

The onset may occur after a trauma or something that threatens their sense of security. This anxiety can also be experienced by some who have been raised in close-knit families where the attachment to significant people is over-emphasized and independence minimized.

"I'm not afraid of leaving my dad. That's not why I don't want to go to school," said Miguel to his therapist. "It's just that he hasn't been doing well since my mother died. I'm afraid the trauma has left him unable to take care of himself. Something might happen to him. He needs me to see him through this tough time."

Seeing his attachment to his dad was extremely hard for Miguel. He had recently experienced a trauma; his mom died. This was certainly something that would prompt any sensitive person to be concerned. Yet Miguel's worry was more than necessary. Although his dad was distressed over the loss of Miguel's mom, he was a very capable man. Therapy helped Miguel to see this. His counselor also helped him to deal with his feelings about his loss. This helped Miguel to have more confidence in himself. After a few months of therapy, Miguel was able to go back to school.

Those who suffer with this disorder can be helped. If you know someone who has been suffering with this problem for more than two weeks, tell him or her to see a professional. Those with separation anxiety can have periods of remission (freedom from the problem) and times when it recurs in the extreme. Finding help is therefore important. Don't assume it has gone away, when, in fact, it is just in a stage of remission.

POST TRAUMATIC STRESS DISORDER (PTSD)

Mary's family had difficulty relating to each other. Frustration was handled physically. When her mother felt frustrated, she was likely to smash some dishes, slam a door, or yell and scream at any family member. Her father often engaged in physical violence with her brother. Since her brother saw his parents reacting in this way, he learned to vent his feelings by striking out. Mary developed a way of protecting herself from her stressful environment by escaping into her room to read. She did this as often as possible. Other times, she avoided her home altogether by getting involved in after-school activities. One day, when Mary was absorbed in a book, her brother threw the door open to her room and began hitting her and yelling at her. He was upset about something that had happened to him and began to blame her. After the incident was over, Mary began to have some strange experiences. Her teacher noticed the difference in her and suggested she see the school psychologist.

In the session, the therapist, Dr. Fleisher, asked Mary questions intended to uncover why she was

One of the symptoms of PTSD is withdrawing from your friends and surroundings because of strong feelings and reactions to an emotional crisis.

having these problems. "Your guidance counselor told me your grades have dropped from a 'B' average down to a 'D.' What do you think the problem is?"

"I don't seem to be as interested in things anymore. I have trouble concentrating and I feel jumpy all the time," said Mary.

"When you have trouble concentrating, what are you thinking about?"

"That's the strange thing," Mary sobbed. "Several weeks ago, I had this fight with my brother. I can't seem to get it out of my mind. I keep going over and over it."

"Tell me, Mary, did your brother hit you?"

"Oh, yes. He was pounding on my head with his fists. That's the part I've been seeing repeatedly in my mind."

The doctor explained to Mary what she was suffering from. "When a traumatic event occurs, it overwhelms the coping mechanisms. Your body and mind are trying very hard to endure the emotional and physical pain. Your whole being is using all of its energy and inner strength to survive. It's as if the event is still happening to you. Your nervous system is on overload. That's why you're not able to put your efforts into normal activity. When this happens, we call it 'Post Traumatic Stress Disorder.'"

Mary learned different types of trauma can cause this disorder. The event can be experienced alone, as in the case of rape or assault, and is often experienced in group situations, such as earthquakes, floods, airplane crashes, large fires, military combat, and car accidents. The disorder can affect someone at any age. In recent years, violence in American schools has increased. Students are attacking classmates as well as teachers. More occurrences of PTSD are being reported by people in these settings, as well.

This syndrome usually shows symptoms within six months of the event and lasts less than six months, but, in some cases, the characteristics of the disorder continue beyond this length of time. When this occurs, the condition is called chronic. War veterans often have chronic PTSD. Soldiers can experience symptoms for many years. Children who grow up in homes where there is constant conflict or trauma may experience PTSD as adults. If the problem is not dealt with therapeutically, they are apt to recreate the same syndrome in their family life with their children.

SCHIZOPHRENIA

Beth's brother Ted had been acting strangely for at least a month. It was most obvious when Ted spoke. If his teacher asked why he was late for class, Ted would reply that Martian time was different from Daylight Saving Time. Ted talked with imaginary persons while walking by himself. His conversations consisted of random comments, with no connection from one thought to the next.

Schizophrenics are often depicted in art as having a "split personality" because their thoughts and statements generally do not relate logically to their behavior.

Beth and Ted were only one year apart and shared many of the same friends and activities at school. As Ted's behavior began to change, however, the kids at school teased Beth about him. Beth had a mixture of emotional reactions. On one hand, she felt embarrassed about the strange way her brother looked and acted. On the other, she felt concern for him.

Ted's parents knew something was seriously wrong, so they decided to consult a psychologist. After the doctor diagnosed Ted as schizophrenic, he suggested a family meeting so he could explain the illness and answer everyone's questions.

"Schizophrenia is a sickness that affects the mind," said the doctor. "It is not the patient's fault that he is ill. It's pretty much like any physical illness. Certain conditions exist both within the person's body/mind and the environment. When a person develops cancer, the cells in various organs become sick and the body can't continue to function normally. The same is true for someone with schizophrenia. The brain is diseased.

"In addition, certain external situations contribute to the problem. There is always an environment of stress and tension. The patient is unable to cope with family problems, for example."

"What do you mean, 'family problems'?" said Beth's dad defensively. "Our family may have a little argument here or there, but we don't have any family problems."

"How would you know, Dad?" said Beth. "You're always working. You don't see what goes on at home most of the time."

Beth's mother started to get nervous. She was torn between protecting her husband from Beth's anger and pacifying her daughter so she wouldn't get too enraged.

"Now Beth, you know your dad has tried to help at home whenever he can." The tension began to increase.

Dr. James interrupted. "It seems there is quite a bit of strain right now in the family."

Dr. James was able to detect stress in the family and bring it to their attention. Ted's illness not only affected him, but his whole family. They were feeling the impact of worrying about Ted and were taking their anxiety out on each other. Their concern about him and frustration of not knowing what to do led them to create even more stress. That's why it is so important to get information about a problem that may be affecting a family member. When a person becomes ill, all those around him or her are in need of help, whether it is a matter of getting some basic information or entering into therapy, too.

Dr. James continued his explanation of schizophrenia to Ted's family.

"Tension itself does not create the problem. You shouldn't blame yourselves. There is a predisposition for schizophrenia. Ted was probably born with this tendency. The family tension, as with all stress, will just add to Ted's difficulties. You might want to come in for a few family sessions to see if you can smooth out some of the issues that create stress in your family, especially now that you have the added strain of Ted's illness."

Ted's family wondered what symptoms to expect. Schizophrenics can have all or some of the following symptoms:

Hallucinations. This is a picture, sound, feeling, taste, or smell that is believed to be real. People with this disease might see someone chasing them with a knife. It is not really happening, but they experience it as if it were real.

Delusions. Delusions are a belief about something that is not true. For example, people with schizophrenia might believe people are trying to poison them with food. The belief can also be a grandiose one. For example, some schizophrenics believe they are Jesus Christ, and can save people.

Appearance. Schizophrenics often have a sloppy appearance. They may dress themselves in odd clothing. In one case, a schizophrenic wore aluminum foil on his head. He believed this allowed him to hear radio waves from Mars. Schizophrenics may go for long periods of time without bathing.

Mood. Schizophrenics' moods are usually based on an internal world that has no relationship to what is going on around them. They may be responding to anger or fear about an imaginary persecutor, but the opposite can also be true. They may believe they are celebrities and experience inappropriate joy. They may speak about something very sad, but their mood appears gleeful.

Speech. Schizophrenics may ramble on and not make any sense at all. Their words may sound disconnected and illogical. Sometimes, their speech is very slow and full of uncomfortable pauses. Sometimes, they won't speak at all.

Onset. The onset of schizophrenia is rarely before late adolescence.

After learning about schizophrenia, Ted's family decided to enter a program designed to help them cope with the problem. Ted also went to therapy. He was given medication to stabilize his symptoms and taught how to manage his stress. He learned that while stress didn't cause his problems, minimizing it would reduce the effect of his symptoms. His parents and sister learned what to expect from Ted. They realized his illness meant there would be certain limitations about how well he would function. They came to accept Ted for who he was and what he could and couldn't do.

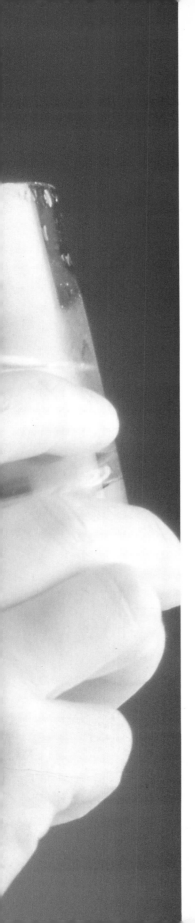

2

SUBSTANCE ABUSE, ALCOHOLISM, AND EATING DISORDERS

By the time I was 18, the disease had a strong grip on me.
I spent the following two years going from unskilled job to
unskilled job. At that point, I was ready and willing to do
whatever it took. So I packed a bag and went to the
hospital the very next day.
—Bob, a recovering alcoholic

Jacqueline started using drugs when her friend Meredith told her they would perk her up. She was feeling sluggish, so Jackie tried some and experienced a noticeable increase in energy. She felt happy and alive and "on top of the world." The next time she took some it was because she had to study for an exam. She remembered how the crystal made her feel last time and thought it seemed like a noble enough reason to want to do well in school. She passed the test with flying colors. For the first time, she received a grade higher than a "C" in math. She wondered if the drug could actually make her smarter. The following three or four occasions when she took stimulants, she made up some equally compelling reasons. She decided she could cope better with the drugs.

Pretty soon, she was taking them so frequently that she couldn't sleep at night. Meredith told her

Alcohol and other drugs are abused by individuals who have
come to depend on their use to mask problems, relieve stress,
or make them feel better. Unfortunately, the more they
abuse, the harder it becomes to cope with life at all.

about some pills that would calm her down enough to get some rest. She tried those and was impressed with the results. She fell asleep as soon as her head hit the pillow. The next day, however, she felt even more groggy and worn out than before she took the original dose of drugs. Now she needed the speed more than ever. The process continued until she was caught up in a vicious cycle. What started out helping her (or so she thought) ended up creating a nightmare. Her ability to function deteriorated. Simply feeling sluggish like she had before she got on the merry-go-round would have been a welcome change from the horror she now lived. She was irritable a good deal of the time. She lost interest in everything except in finding money and ways to get more drugs.

Jacqueline's drug use began innocently enough. She just needed a little energy to get through the day, but she got caught up by the drug's seductive nature. All abusers begin with a rational reason that makes perfectly good sense to them at the time. Teenagers who see their parents use alcohol to make them feel better believe it's okay to use drugs in the same way. "It's just recreational use," they say, but what begins as entertainment often ends up as much fun as playing in quicksand.

Those who abuse drugs usually end up taking larger doses more frequently in order to obtain the same high again and again.

Chemicals that alter mood or behavior and affect the central nervous system are the most commonly abused. Mood changes can be of a calming or sedative nature, or stimulating and uplifting. Often, the user alternates between tranquilizing drugs and ones that arouse the system.

The need for drugs is sometimes valid. Taking medication with a doctor's guidance can solve some problems. Jacqueline demonstrated a need for this type of therapy. Her symptoms were those of a person suffering from depression. Her effort to deal with her mood by using street drugs is all too common. Many people with substance-abuse disorders are attempting to self-medicate their problems.

Several patterns of use can be categorized as substance abuse. Users who don't indulge on a daily basis or who aren't intoxicated throughout the day find it difficult to see themselves as having a substance abuse problem. People with the inability to cut down, no matter how infrequently they use drugs, however, are considered to have a drug problem. A teen may take drugs only on weekends or just with certain individuals. If he finds he is unable to say no in those instances, he has a drug problem. If a user has to plan ahead to restrict his intake to certain times of the day, he has a drug problem. Needing the substance just to function is clear cut evidence of a drug problem.

When greater amounts of the substance are needed to achieve the desired effect, users have developed a tolerance. In other words, their bodies can withstand the original dosage without feeling the same results. It then becomes necessary to take more in order to get the same high. The same is true if there is a diminished effect with regular use of the same dose.

Dependence occurs when a tolerance to the dosage is developed. Withdrawal—a painful physical reaction—is the result when a user is deprived of the drug. Some withdrawal symptoms include:

- Flu-like symptoms, such as vomiting, sweats, chills, joint and bone aches
- Racing or paranoid thoughts (thinking someone is talking about you or "after" you)

- Nightmares and/or an inability to sleep
- Loss of appetite
- Inability to sit still
- Hallucinations
- Irrational fears

FIVE MAJOR CONCERNS OF TEENS

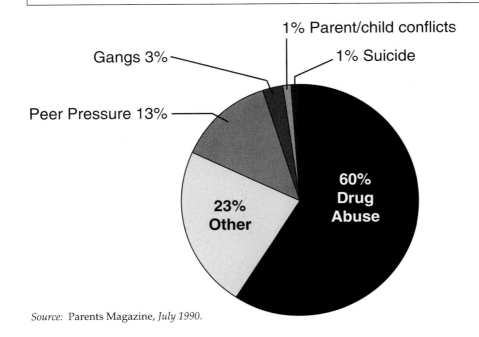

Source: Parents Magazine, July 1990.

Substance abuse usually begins in the adolescent years. When the disorder begins early in life, a lifelong pattern of low achievement often results. Individuals tend to work in a field far below their abilities. They might end up with jobs as laborers, when, in fact, their mental capacity is far superior. They may go from job to job because of their frustration in not being able to fulfill their potential. Severe emotional disorders can result. They may suffer from hallucinations for the rest of their lives, or they may develop delusions.

ALCOHOLISM

"Can't you see how your drinking is ruining your life?" Mr. Wargo asked his son.

"So I have a few drinks on weekends with some friends," replied Jonathan. "I'm just trying to have a little fun. That's not so bad."

Drinking and driving is one of the top causes of death among young people in the United States. Alcoholism is a sign of deep emotional problems.

"What about the car you wrecked when you and your friends were having a few drinks and a little fun?"

"It was just an accident. I'm not the only one who has ever had a fender bender."

"It wasn't just a fender bender, Jonathan. You nearly demolished the car. Besides, it wasn't simply an accident. It was an accident while you were under the influence of alcohol."

"I'm sorry, Dad. I won't drink and drive again."

The single most difficult symptom to treat in alcoholism is denial. Denial is a defense mechanism in which the alcoholic will not admit he has a problem. Even when presented with clear evidence that the disease exists, the sufferer rationalizes it away.

Sometimes, denying the existence of the problem is easy because the drinker believes one must get drunk every day to be considered an actual alcoholic. Jonathan drank only on weekends. He didn't understand this was one of several patterns of drinking indicating he had an alcohol problem. An addict may drink only periodically, yet still clearly demonstrate that the disease is present. He may have periods of sobriety (times of not drinking at all), and then go on binges (periods of continuous, uncontrollable drinking). The sober times can last months and even years. The drinking pattern is only one indication of the illness.

OTHER SYMPTOMS OF ALCOHOLISM

Along with denial and the inability to cut down or stop consuming alcohol, drinking interferes with the normal day-to-day activities of life. Sometimes, an individual misses school or work because of his drinking. This may be because he is intoxicated at the time he is expected to perform his responsibilities and can't quite function. It can also happen because his self-esteem is low as a result of feeling bad about himself after his last encounter with drinking. Often, alcohol abuse leads to antisocial behavior while intoxicated, such as angry outbursts. An addict's personality can be filled with rage, and outbursts can occur even when he is not drinking. This is known as "practicing his disease." Jonathan was known to pick fights with his friends and display other forms of violence during the week, even though he kept his drinking confined to weekends.

Jonathan's sister, Alicia, was quite concerned about his behavior. She'd always had little fights with him. He'd complain about not getting a borrowed item back or she'd object to his using the family car when she wanted it. This was basically normal brother and sister stuff, but lately, things were different. He was furious with her for no apparent reason. When a reason for his anger did exist, it was clearly out of proportion to the cause. Alicia was becoming frightened of him during his fits of rage. This fear affected her to such a degree that she began to avoid him. Anger towards him began to develop that started to affect the genuine love she'd always felt for him. There was a mixture of emotions that confused her.

CARING FOR AN ALCOHOLIC

One day, Alicia and her father were talking about Jonathan and the change in his behavior. She explained about the effect it was having on her. Mr. Wargo shared her concern and decided to seek some help. He'd already met Bob, a recovering alcoholic from Alcoholics Anonymous (AA), a 12-step program, and used him as a resource. Bob told him about a program for friends and families of people who had the disorder.

Bob explained that alcoholism is a family disease. The addict has the obvious drinking problem, but what is not so obvious is how the significant people in the addict's life contribute to the continuation of the disease. Anyone who does this is called an enabler. This is not something people do deliberately or with awareness. An enabler cares a great deal for the sufferer, and certainly wouldn't want to consciously harm him or her, but nevertheless allows the abuser to continue the abuse.

Alicia and her father were both encouraged and disappointed, so Bob told them about various places to get help. He told them about a group called Al-Anon. This national organization is made up of people who have a friend or family member suffering from the sickness. Meetings are held every week, and even daily in some places. Al-Anon has discussions that help people see they are not alone. At each meeting, they see how others have dealt with the situation, and they can find literature that explains how the disease works. Then, depending upon how severe the alcoholic's problem is, the family may want to consider a hospital program as well. Most have inpatient and outpatient programs that don't just treat the alcoholic, but also include a family recovery program.

RECOGNIZING ALCOHOLISM

Bob also described his own battle with the bottle. "I started drinking when I was a teenager," he said. "But the real story began when I watched my father die from the disease. I was only about 12 years old when I saw how deadly and devastating this sickness can be. He'd been drinking for many years. The doctor told him countless times that his drinking was literally killing him. In fact, two years before he died, the doctor gave him only about a year or so to live. His denial of his sickness was so strong he wouldn't stop even after that. I loved my father very much and it was very difficult to watch him suffer. The last two years of his life caused me tremendous pain. When he finally died, I was emotionally destroyed. I stopped caring about myself. Nothing in life mattered much. I began to drink just as my father had. I'd been thrown out of school by the time I was 16. By the time I was 18, the disease had a strong grip on me. I spent the following two years going from unskilled job to unskilled job.

"It was like a ghost was chasing me. I felt if I stayed in one place too long, it might catch up with me and scare me. I was lucky my aunt loved me through these times. She helped my dad raise me from the time I was three years old. I continued to live with her through my four years of hell. She tried to help me, but I only slapped the hand she extended to me.

"One day, I came home from another job from which I'd been fired and saw her sitting in a chair in the kitchen. She tried hard not to show her emotions, but I could see something in her face. The ghost finally caught up to me. The way her face looked reminded me of the way I felt four years earlier when I watched my father die. All the sorrow of watching him left me with a raw and burning ache in my chest. I had spent the last four years trying to drink the feeling away. Now the look in my aunt's face brought it all back to me. She was watching me do to myself what I saw my father do to himself. And for just a moment, long enough to get beyond my own self-centeredness, I felt my aunt's pain. Then I knew I had to do something.

"I called our family doctor. He remembered me from the many times I brought my father to see him. I told him I was having the same problem as my dad and I needed help. Dr. Martin explained that I needed to detoxify, so my body could get rid of the poisons that were building up in my system from the alcohol. I went to the hospital the next day."

Bob and other alcoholics find it is difficult to help themselves when they're in the midst of it all. "The first step is the hardest. If you have any strength at all, even if you have to crawl, call Alcoholics Anonymous, the local hospital, your family doctor, or even a counselor at school. Believe me, it's worth doing."

Bob's case was a little unusual. He was able to break through his denial on his own and admit he had a problem. If you feel you have a problem, or know someone else who does, get help. What will help one person may not help another. There are places you can contact listed in the back of this book. Members of AA recommend you attend at least six meetings before you decide if it is or is not for you. Because denial is always at work on one level or another, the tendency is to find things in one particular meeting that aren't quite right. You may use an excuse to discount the entire program. For example, the personalities may not be those with whom you would normally choose to associate. Therefore, going to several meetings will help you find at least something or someone to identify with. Taking the first step is often frightening and difficult to take. It can be useful to ask a trusted friend or family member to accompany you.

Individual counseling or psychotherapy may be a useful addition to a program specifically designed for addiction. Alcoholics have many problems dealing with life itself, and the therapy can help the individual deal with these issues.

Hypnotherapy is also an effective therapy to be used in addition to other types of help. Hypnosis can help with the issues directly related to stopping the actual compulsive or uncontrollable act. It can help with impulse control, stress reduction, and self-esteem.

Chad sought the help of a hypnotherapist. He knew he was an alcoholic. He couldn't stop drinking no matter how hard he tried. His ability to do his school work had deteriorated. He was desperate. His strong motivation to conquer his drinking was reinforced by family support. His brothers and sisters were ready and willing to offer the help he might need. His hypnotherapist designed a program of recovery. She helped him to deter his need to drink by reinforcing other positive behavior that replaced drinking. She offered suggestions to help him cope with anxious situations. She taught him self-hypnosis and other techniques to help him relieve stress. Chad was successful at using these techniques.

Within six weeks, he quit drinking entirely. Once he stopped his abusive behavior, however, other problems emerged. He discovered he had a problem sleeping. Within a short period of time, he developed severe phobias and panic attacks. These were all problems that existed before, but were covered up by his drinking. Once they surfaced, hypnotherapy was then applied to these underlying problems.

Chad was an unusual case. Getting more help than private therapy can offer is often necessary. Groups such as AA or hospital programs offer continued ongoing support. Chad was highly motivated and was able to utilize his therapy to his advantage. His family's support provided him with the edge he needed to rise above his problem.

EATING DISORDERS

Colleen had always done well in school. In fact, she did well in everything she tried. She was even the star performer of her dance school. Her parents provided her with many material needs that others envied. Colleen was very aware of having come from an advantaged background. As a result, she felt pressure to show her appreciation and meet the high expectations of her teachers and parents. At age 16, she graduated and was accepted into a good college.

Young persons with eating disorders all have one thing in common: They are obsessed with their weight and physique, and depend too much on their appearance to boost their self-esteem.

She was terrified of not doing well and began to put herself under incredible pressure. Out of stress, she began to develop strange eating patterns. At first, she ate small amounts of food at meal time—about half of her normal portion size. In a very short time, she ate practically nothing. She started to lose a great deal of weight. In one year's time, she went from 118 pounds to 84 pounds. Colleen's disorder is called anorexia nervosa.

Caryn withdraws from activities and friends so she can engage in binge eating. She may eat an entire cake at one time or eat several meals within a short period of time. It is always done secretly. She always feels guilty and remorseful afterward. She feels like she cannot control this behavior. She is very unhappy about being 30 pounds overweight. Her weight affects the way she lives. She wants to go to school dances, but feels she needs to wait until she gets thinner. There are many other activities she denies herself because of her appearance. Caryn is a compulsive eater.

Susan has many of the same eating patterns as Caryn, but she is not overweight. She is, however, very concerned about becoming overweight. She learned about purging. After each binge, she vomits and has been able to remain at a normal weight. She knows of someone else who takes laxatives after a binge so she won't gain weight. Susan innocently tried purging, not realizing she would get caught up in it and not be able to stop. At first, she binged and purged once a month. Now she practices this compulsion every day. Susan is bulimic.

Each of these girls has an eating disorder. Although the symptoms and consequences vary, they really involve emotional problems even though they seem to be physical ones.

FOOD OBSESSIONS

An obsession is an abnormal amount of time spent thinking about one idea or set of ideas. Both Susan and Caryn use a lot of their time focusing on food. They plan for times when they can be alone and binge. They might even manipulate the situation they're in so they can eat in private. For example, they both refrain from eating much at a party and offer to help clean up after everyone is gone. Then they eat everything they can get their hands on. Caryn often offers to run an errand for her mother. She then uses the opportunity to buy food and shovel it into her mouth as fast as she can. Both girls spend an excessive amount of time thinking about and planning for their cravings for unusual amounts of food. Although Colleen hardly eats at all, the same mechanism is at work. Her obsession is with not eating. It is the opposite side of the same coin. She forces herself to avoid food. It takes an awful lot of obsessive thinking about food to consciously keep away from it.

Both Susan and Caryn feel unable to control their food intake. In Colleen's case, she is so frightened she won't be able to control her eating that she overcompensates by restricting herself in the extreme. The unusual amount of weight loss makes it apparent something is wrong, however. Whenever Colleen's mother asks her about her changing body, she becomes even more guarded and controlled. She takes up more of her time and thought processes to avoid eating and give the impression that nothing is wrong.

One time, when her mother confronted her, Colleen answered, "I ate after school." Then she dashed up the stairs to her room in an attempt to avoid any more questions.

Mrs. Avery followed her daughter upstairs. "What did you eat? When did you eat?" she persisted in a worried voice.

"A bunch of us went over to the fast food place. I had a hamburger and fries and a coke," Colleen lied in an effort to keep her mother off her back. She had to avoid sitting at the dinner table with her family so they wouldn't see that she wasn't really eating much at all. Colleen spent more and more of her time manipulating situations so she could protect her secret.

BODY IMAGE

In each example of these emotional disorders, an obsessive amount of attention is placed on body image. For instance, Colleen was afraid of being fat. Her view of herself was unrealistic. When she was at her normal weight, she felt fat. No matter how much weight she lost, she believed it was never enough, even though at 84

Anorexics look in the mirror and are convinced they see a "fat" person.

pounds, her body looked like a skeleton. Her ribs stuck out and counting each rib was easy, even from a distance. Her shoulder blades jutted out of her body. Her hair began to fall out. Despite all of this, she still refused to eat. Her family finally had to admit her to an in-patient hospital program for people with eating disorders.

Susan's obsession with her weight and body image is equally strong. She, too, feels afraid of getting fat and will avoid it at all costs; she is even willing to pay with her health. Caryn is constantly berating herself for being fat. Although she is overweight, her image of herself is out of proportion. She sees herself as grotesque. Both she and Susan realized they had eating disorders and decided to seek out a self-help program called Overeaters Anonymous (OA).

WHO IS SUSCEPTIBLE?

Most people who suffer from eating disorders are young women. Some young men are affected, but this is less common. The onset of the disease is usually between the ages of 14 and 16. The illness begins at a time when pressures are at an all-time high. Women in particular feel pressure to be thin and attractive. Some feel they are only as good as their appearance.

A young woman's emerging sexuality creates confusion for some and fear for others. These feelings often contribute to these problems developing. Many factors make up the profile of someone with anorexia, bulimia, or compulsive eating. Typical traits among all three are perfectionism, a high-strung personality, and a tendency to prefer isolation.

Overeaters Anonymous (OA) defines compulsive eating as a three-fold disease; one that is spiritual, emotional, and physical. Psychologists have additional theories about the psychological component, but they, too, accept many of the OA philosophies. Some experts believe there is an underlying depression in those who suffer from this disorder. It is not clear, however, whether the eating disorder caused the depression or the depression existed first and caused the eating disorder.

Eating disorders are never totally cured. The problems go into remission; that is, they go into an inactive state. People with these problems can live normal lives provided they accept that the tendency for their problems is always there. Once they resign themselves to this fact, it will remind them how important it is to use techniques to help themselves throughout the rest of their lives. Whether the tools they practice are behavioral techniques, communication skills, or spiritual philosophies, these tools will provide a basis for recovery.

ARE YOU A COMPULSIVE EATER?

The following questions ask you to rate your own unhappiness and other feelings regarding your eating behavior. If you answer "Yes" to several of them, and suspect that you have an eating disorder, seek help.

Statement	*Answer*	
I eat in order to deal with all kinds of feelings: happiness, sadness, boredom, excitement, etc.	Yes ☑	No ☐
Overeating makes me unhappy.	Yes ☐	No ☑
My eating habits interfere with my social life. My social life revolves around food.	Yes ☑	No ☐
I eat normally in front of others, but binge when I am alone.	Yes ☐	No ☑
I daydream in school because I am thinking about food or about losing weight.	Yes ☐	No ☑
I sometimes steal food or steal money to buy food.	Yes ☐	No ☑
I spend more money than I would like to on junk food, no matter how much I try to stop.	Yes ☑	No ☐

3

WHAT CAUSES EMOTIONAL DISORDERS?

What other dungeon is so dark as one's heart! What jailer so inexorable as one's self!
—Nathaniel Hawthorne, *The House of Seven Gables*

Jessica and David were camping in Yosemite. They had returned to their tent after a long, exhausting hike. They were relaxing, enjoying the scenery and cooking a meal. Their walk created a big appetite. Suddenly, a huge brown bear appeared in front of them. Jessica was so overcome by fear that she froze. Her heart began to beat fast. Her hunger vanished. She and David experienced a surge of energy caused by adrenaline, a hormone that gives the body power. When the bear moved away, they both ran faster than either of them thought possible.

Human beings have a built-in system that gives them extraordinary energy during times of stress. The body prepares itself to fight danger or run from it. This is called the "fight or flight" response. During times of fright, those bodily systems needed to deal with danger are enhanced, while those functions that are not needed are temporarily bypassed. Jessica and David's hunger vanished. Their bodies concentrated on energy needed to keep them running at a pace fast enough to escape the danger. These processes helped human beings survive in the wild when danger was a matter of life or death.

Fear triggers a reaction in our brains, which in turn sends the body into action with a temporarily high dose of adrenaline.

Stressful events cause the body to trigger these same physiological responses. In fact, any change, no matter how small, can create stress. For some, even simple, everyday occurrences can stimulate stress. Getting a haircut, deciding on a perfect outfit to wear to a special event, simply driving a car, or getting a new job all produce stress. What happens in modern society when the stress response is activated, but the energy is not used in an active way? Let's say Jill gets a "D" on an exam. She knows it won't go over well with her parents. They might reprimand or punish her. At the very least, she expects they will disapprove. This triggers the danger response that gets her body physically ready to act. Yet no actual harm is threatening her body; the stress has nowhere to go. In time, the stress builds up if appropriate outlets are not found.

HEALTHY OUTLETS FOR STRESS

A person can react to stress in many ways. One way is for Jill to take action and put her energy into studying more and applying herself at school. When confronted by upset parents, she accepts responsibility for her actions and sees her parents' response as valid. Her self-esteem is intact enough to allow for having made a mistake. She simply picks herself up and moves on. The stress, therefore, will not build up or cause problems.

Jogging, bicycling, dancing, cooking—doing any physical activity that you enjoy is an excellent way to reduce stress and tension in your life.

Sometimes, people react to stress with emotion. One person might become angry with herself for not meeting expectations, or direct her anger externally toward her parents. She may not be able to maintain as much objectivity as Jill. Yet there are other outlets for this stress that are equally successful at helping us cope. For example, Rob failed the same test as Jill, but he released his anger by grabbing a basketball and going to the nearest court to throw the ball around. He cursed at the ball when it didn't go into the hoop. He ran up one side of the court and down the other, all the while beating at the ball as if it was responsible for doing poorly on the test. After an hour of such rigorous activity, he fell down exhausted. Suddenly, he saw things differently. This was just one test. He knew he could earn some extra credit and bring his grade point average back up. Good feelings began to come back and he was then able to enjoy the rest of his day. His ability to function was restored, and his emotions never got out of hand.

UNHEALTHY ATTEMPTS TO DEAL WITH STRESS

What happens when people don't use constructive outlets for stress? Some people let situations get the best of them. They immediately respond with a feeling of helplessness. They feel that life does things to them and that they are victims. It is true that some people receive more than their share of problems to deal with in life. They may not have the support of friends or family around them to help in dealing with these troubles, and they may not have the emotional stability to cope by themselves.

These factors may push the individual into deeper despair, and the vicious cycle continues. When a person is overly stressed, the ability to cope with unfortunate conditions is further weakened. During these times, we may choose unhealthy outlets in an effort to cope. Alcohol and substance abuse may find their way into our lives. Other behavior problems may be used to vent tension. Some of these may include: truancy, getting into fights, stealing, unsatisfying sexual relationships with many partners, and unwanted pregnancy.

DYSFUNCTIONAL RELATIONSHIPS

Robert was an only child. He was the focus of attention in his family and usually received more than he wanted. His love for baseball was sabotaged when his father participated a little too much. He showed Robert exactly how to hold the bat. When Robert swung at the ball, his father corrected him. He went through every last detail of every aspect of the game showing his son the best way to do it. Robert was never allowed to learn for himself. His mother also did everything for him. If Robert forgot his baseball mitt before a game, she'd go running back home to get it rather than let him suffer the consequences of his actions. Robert's self-esteem was suffering. He felt like he couldn't do anything right. He began to feel resentment toward his parents.

Dysfunction can occur even with the best of intentions. Robert's parents certainly cared about him, but the way they expressed their love interfered with his natural process of growing and learning. Robert knew his mother and father loved him. This made it even more difficult to understand his feelings. He believed expressing some of his negative emotions would hurt his parents, so he remained silent while his feelings festered.

Good relationships serve many purposes. They provide a bond that gives people a sense of support and belonging. This bond is another form of communication. Some relationships are dysfunctional. The balance of give and take is disrupted. An unequal share of responsibility falls on one person's shoulders. Resentments build up inside and lack an outlet. In many cases, the people involved aren't aware of the underlying feeling. They may deny their existence or simply be so completely involved in trying to carry their burdens that they don't take the time to notice their internal world.

Resentments are not only felt by the person carrying the extra load. The reason for these feelings is clear, but the one who allows this pattern to continue may harbor bad feelings as well. He or she may feel at a loss as to how to participate more. The feeling of being dominated by the other person may interfere with the ability to contribute his or her fair share to the relationship.

Such dysfunction can occur when there is a physical or emotional illness. The healthy members of the family are then left to pick up the slack. Dysfunction can occur in single-parent homes, where the demands of life require the adult to do more than he or she is able. This may leave older children with the burden of caring for younger siblings, or an only child may be left to care for himself in ways for which he is not quite ready.

A dysfunction is created when a person is not able to fulfill the normal responsibilities of his position and role in life. Sometimes, the demand does not come from external circumstances. It can appear when internal conflicts and unresolved problems dominate the individual's attention. For example, Michael was raised in foster homes. He was sexually molested by his foster father when he was ten years old. He never told anyone of the incident. Shortly after the episode, he was moved to another foster home. He believed the problem was behind him and went on to live his life, never giving the situation another thought.

After college, he married a woman he loved very much. Having a family was important to the couple, so they had two children. Michael had a job he enjoyed. Everything in his life was going rather well, until one day he was plagued with thoughts about molesting children. He couldn't understand this. The thoughts seemed to come from nowhere. They disrupted his work and family. He was so ashamed, he began to withdraw into himself. His relationship with his children began to suffer. He wasn't able to give them the time and attention they needed.

When he tried to become involved with their activities, he was preoccupied with his own troubles. Over the course of several years, his participation as a father deteriorated to a harmful degree.

After many years of unnecessary suffering, he finally sought therapy and learned why he was preoccupied with this negativity. The therapist explained how people will try to work out disturbances of their childhood by recreating the same behaviors in adulthood. Fortunately, Michael was able to resist the impulse to do to other children what had been done to him. The unfortunate part was that it took so much mental and emotional energy that he was unable to fulfill his responsibilities. His children suffered the loss. They grew up in a home with a dysfunctional father. From the outside, it appeared normal enough. The children had a mother and father who loved them. They were given enough food and clothing and lived in a comfortable house in a middle-class neighborhood. It took a closer look to see where the dysfunction had seeped in.

ALCOHOLISM

Alcoholism is sometimes the cause of a family's dysfunction. It takes a great deal of time and energy to deal with the unusual needs of drinking. It becomes a preoccupation of the person who suffers. When a parent is an alcoholic, it greatly interferes with his or her ability to perform as a parent.

Elly's mom was an alcoholic, and her dad lived in another state and saw her only about once a year. At the age of 14, she was often called upon to take adult responsibilities. Her mom went on bouts of drinking and neglected taking care of bills and other household obligations. Her mom regularly received notices that the gas and electricity would be shut off if the bill wasn't paid. Her mother was too involved in her disease to notice. Elly had to take charge and make sure the bill was paid. She had the additional responsibility of preparing meals for herself and her little brother.

She'd come home from school and find her mother in the bedroom watching television or sleeping, too intoxicated to do anything. She'd give her brother a bath, read him a story, and virtually take on all the tasks a parent should do. Her mom had another binge the night her brother's tooth fell out. Elly decided to stay up late, until after her brother was fast asleep, so she could play tooth fairy. She was put in a position of protecting her brother from needless disappointment, something her parents should have been there to do.

Scientists have not identified a single cause for manic-depression. Some mood swings may be hereditary, or caused by chemical differences in key areas of the brain that control behavior.

Although it was a very caring and responsible thing for her to do, it created a hardship for Elly when she was already trying to deal with her own problems. Children should not be expected to make adult decisions that require life experience, yet kids in Elly's position are constantly being called upon to use their judgment, however limited that may be. This stunts their emotional growth and can create problems for them later.

CHEMICAL IMBALANCES AND HEREDITY

Research shows some emotional disorders can be attributed to brain chemistry imbalances. The body chemistry of a manic-depressive is distinctly different from that of a person without this problem. One experiment has shown that people with this disorder have a lower level of brain-wave activity in certain areas of their brain. These include the areas that organize and inhibit behavior, and control personality, judgment, and future planning. For example, it is possible that when a manic-depressive behaves without regard to consequences, his lack of control is because his brain is not functioning with the proper amount of energy to the part that normally restricts this activity. Further studies are being done to determine if there is an actual genetic difference (that is, a hereditary cause) in the chromosomes to account for this chemical imbalance. There may be a blueprint in the part of the cell that passes along certain traits from one generation to another. Other ideas being investigated involve the effect emotional attitude and stress have on changing brain chemistry. More and more studies show how our own thoughts can play a major role in producing chemical reactions in our bodies.

TRANSITIONAL PERIODS

Everyone has times in his or her life that tend to be more stressful than others. These are usually periods of change or loss. If a person lacks a strong emotional capacity to deal with life's changes, these transitional times compound problems. Illness is one stressful time. The loss of a friend or family member through death or a boyfriend or girlfriend through break-up all add additional stress to the normal day-to-day tensions of life. Moving to a new neighborhood, graduating from school, or a parent's remarriage are transitional periods of life that also create extra tensions.

Even joyful changes create stress. Essie was looking forward to graduating from high school. Her parents promised her a trip to Europe the summer before she started college. As the day of the big event grew closer, Essie felt a strange tension in her chest. At times, her heart would even race. She had doubts about her desire to go abroad. At other times, she felt a sense of excitement at the prospect. Even though the occasion was a happy one, a degree of stress about the unknown was apt to sneak in.

Moving is one of life's more common events that can increase stress.

Essie rode out the highs and lows. When she experienced excitement, she permitted herself to feel joy. When she experienced negative feelings of the unknown, she let herself feel those emotions as well. She didn't try to change them or tell herself she was being silly. Her ability to adapt to her changing environment and her varying feelings gave her the tools she needed to cope with her stress.

WHEN SOMEONE YOU LOVE HAS AN EMOTIONAL DISORDER

When a loved one has an emotional disorder, knowing how to handle it is difficult. There is a mix of loving emotions and negative ones. A person may empathize with the pain someone is in, yet feel resentful, too. If the illness afflicts a sibling, it may seem like he or she is getting all the time and attention from the parents. If it is a parent, a teenager may feel the tables are turned unfairly. The youngster may have to take on the responsibilities of an adult. Since the one with the disorder temporarily loses his or her ability to be entirely functional, there will be an unequal aspect to their relationships. For example, the young person may have to ensure that younger siblings are cared for properly. Preparing dinner, helping them get ready for school, and staying home to babysit may all fall into the realm of new responsibilities. This will take a great deal of understanding of the sick family member as well as understanding one's own needs.

One of the most trying emotional traumas for the one who is not ill is to free him- or herself of guilt for being healthy. This is sometimes called "survivor's guilt." While letting the person in pain know of the healthy person's interest and concern is important, it is just as important for the healthy person to realize he or she is human. Airlines explain this in their own way each time they take passengers from one place to another. Before takeoff, the flight attendant describes how to use the oxygen mask should it become necessary. The attendant explains that if an adult is with a small child, that adult should put his or her own oxygen mask on first, then put the youngster's on. If the reverse is tried, the adult may lose consciousness while trying to take care of the child, and both of them may be harmed. In other words, the adult can't help others unless he or she takes care of him- or herself first.

Carrie's mother suffered from depression. This put a great deal of strain on the rest of the family. Her father expected her to come home from school and do household chores before her homework. After her schoolwork, she was to help her little brother Jim with his. On weekends, she was relied upon to do the bookkeeping for the family business, a job her mother did before her illness. There was no time for Carrie's friends or hobbies. She began to resent her mother.

STRESS

Everyday stress is compounded by certain events in life that have an unusually devastating effect. Dr. Thomas Holmes and Dr. Richard Rahe have developed a scale rating common life events that cause varying degrees of stress. When a number of events occur in a short period of time—even good ones—an individual's stress level is increased. The Life Event Scale was originally created for adults and the circumstances they are likely to encounter. The following scale was adapted to those events an adolescent is apt to experience.

Circle the events that apply to you in the past six months. Then circle the events that apply to you in the past year. Total both of your scores, then consult the scale to determine your stress level.

LIFE EVENT SCALE

Life Event	Value	Life Event	Value
Death of a parent	100	Sibling moving out of the house	29
Divorce or separation of parents	73	Family arguments with grandparents	28
Parent's jail term	65	Winning school or community awards	26
Jail or detention center for self	65	Parent or primary caretaker stopping or starting work	26
Death of close family member (grandparent)	63	School starting or ending	26
Personal injury or illness	53	Change in family's living standards	25
Parent's remarriage	50	Change in personal habits (bedtime, homework, etc.)	24
Expulsion from school	50	Trouble with parents	
Suspension from school	47	(lack of communication)	23
Parents getting back together	45	Change in school hours or schedule	20
Long vacation (Christmas, summer)	45	Family move	20
Parent's illness	44	A new school	20
Mother's pregnancy	40	New sports, hobbies, family recreation activities	19
Anxiety about sex	39	Change in church or temple activities	19
Birth of a new sibling	39	Change in social activities;	
New school, new classroom, or new teacher	39	new friends, loss of old ones, peer pressure	18
Parents' money problems	38	Change in sleeping habits	16
Death or moving away of a close friend	38	Change in number of family get-togethers	15
Change in school curriculum	37	Change in eating habits	15
More fights with parents, or parents fighting more	35	Breaking school, home, or community rules	11
Change in school or home responsibilities	29		

STRESS SCALE

Score	Stress Level	
150-199	Moderate	37%
200-299	Medium	51%
300 or more	Severe	79%

If your score indicates you have severe stress, you might want to ask your parent if you can consult a therapist. If your score indicates you have moderate stress, you might want to learn some stress-reduction techniques. These can be learned from a book or a course at a local college.

When one family member experiences severe emotional or physical problems, the other family members can either provide comfort or begin to resent the constant demands of helping the other person cope.

Dealing with resentment is not easy. It's like hitting someone when he or she is down. If you are feeling resentment, you probably are afraid to express your feelings. The best way to deal with these feelings is to realize the sickness is the enemy—not the person who is ill. It may be easier to acknowledge your resentment when it is redirected in this way.

In a short while, Carrie began to get worn out. She saw her father work very hard, too, and didn't want to complain about her added responsibilities. She began to display her own symptoms of a minor depression. She was exhausted and beginning to have difficulty sleeping. Not until after Carrie also showed signs of becoming depressed was attention paid to her needs. When Carrie began to suffer from the same symptoms as her mother, her father realized he was depending upon her more than was healthy.

The two of them discussed alternatives. They were able to set priorities for all that needed to be done. Carrie's health was more important than getting all of the work done. A bookkeeper was hired to help with the business. Three times a week, they went out to dinner or brought in prepared meals from the restaurant. This allowed Carrie free time to do some relaxing and enjoyable activities. In a short while, she was back to normal. She was able to function in a positive, capable way in all of her responsibilities.

HOW TO GET THEM INTO TREATMENT

People with emotional disorders need professional help; however, they may not want it and refuse it outright. First, it is human nature to want to keep things the way they are because it is comfortable. Second, illness is bad, and people don't want to be associated with something bad, so they deny that it's real. The combination of longing for the familiar and denying illness creates a resistance to treatment. The sick people are hurting and want to keep others away from them. They may become very defensive when approached about their problem. Getting beyond the emotional walls sick people can build is quite a task.

Sick people may continue to spiral down deeper into the sickness and not even know it. If you know people like this, show concern and respect for them. Recognize that it is illness, not weakness. When they see that you care, it may break through enough of the barriers to allow them to accept help. Remember, an emotional disorder develops when people feel they are not important enough for others to care about. Their self-esteem is so low, they may believe they are unworthy of love.

Help is essential. The first step may be talking to a school counselor, nurse, or teacher. Often, clergy are schooled in therapy and counseling and are able to help. If not, they can probably direct you to other resources for assistance. A trusted family friend may supply the support you need to help you cope with the situation.

If you think you have an emotional problem, the same things apply. The problem won't go away by itself, so the only way is to seek help, difficult as it may be. Telling someone your problems is not easy. Find someone you can trust. A family friend or sibling may be able to give you guidance, or help you to tell your parents. Make up your mind to take the first step. It will undoubtedly take courage. Talk to yourself. Give yourself a pep talk. Tell yourself you can do it. You will be surprised at how effective this can be.

4

HANDLING DEPRESSION AND ANXIETY

When down in the mouth, remember Jonah.
He came out all right.
—Thomas Edison

Marge loved skiing. She looked forward to every opportunity to enjoy the sport. One day, her mother gave her a birthday card. She opened it expecting to see a typical mushy poem about how much she was loved. This time when she opened the envelope, she was pleasantly surprised to see two tickets to a weekend at her favorite resort. Her heart started to beat fast with excitement. Adrenaline surged through her body, giving her a boost of energy. She was happy, and anyone observing her knew it, too.

The next month, Marge was riding a chair lift at the ski resort. She and her friend were sitting calmly as the lift slowly rose up the steep mountain-side. Suddenly, the lift came to an abrupt halt, and the minutes crept by while Marge and her friend got colder in the still mountain air. Being stranded on the lift at such a height bothered Marge. Her heart started to beat very fast. A rush of adrenaline surged through her body even as the chair lift refused to move. She was scared, and anyone observing her knew it, too.

In these instances, two widely different events triggered the same physical response. What was different was Marge's emotional reaction to each situation. In one, she interpreted the circumstances

Certain situations, events, and places can trigger anxiety.
Anxiety is a state of restlessness or agitation that can cause
uneasiness and even physical symptoms such as chest pains.

as frightening. She may have thought, "I could fall from this chair lift and die." She could see a mental picture of herself lying on the ground critically injured. She may have imagined herself in pain, waiting for someone to rescue her. Such images and thoughts naturally create a feeling of fear, but the receipt of the skiing tickets conjured up pictures and thoughts that created happy feelings. Marge imagined the thrill of zooming down the slopes again. She may have seen a mental picture of herself on skis, the wind in her face, and the sensation of moving over the powdery snow.

Nothing in the nature of any event like those above makes it good or bad. The individual places a value judgment on them. A different person experiencing the same two events as Marge may have a different reaction. Someone who enjoys flying or hang gliding may have enjoyed the view from a ski lift so she could photograph the winter scenery. On the other hand, the prospect of sliding down a slippery mountain on two sticks at high speed might instill fear in her. Our thoughts—our ability to imagine—influence our emotions at just such times.

This is not just theory. Scientific research has found specific chemical reactions in the body that are triggered by our mental processes. Our bodies produce chemicals that are responsible for creating these varied feelings. Why is this important? It gives each of us more power and control over our feelings than we may have believed possible. A person in the moderate or mild stages of a depression or anxiety has a great deal of influence over the experience. Someone who is deeper in emotional distress will need professional help. He or she will, however, greatly improve the progress of the recovery by using techniques that trigger positive chemical reactions.

CREATING POSITIVE CONDITIONS

Science is uncovering more and more evidence about the effects of our minds on the progression of illness. One amazing example is a man named Norman Cousins who recovered from a debilitating heart attack through the use of his mental efforts. His condition was so severe, doctors couldn't operate on him. They viewed his case as hopeless. Cousins refused to accept their diagnosis. His will to live was so strong he was able to use his mind to help set the body's healing powers in motion. He checked himself out of the hospital and into a hotel room armed with dozens of humorous movies and books. He literally laughed himself back to health.

After his recovery, Cousins wrote many books. They detail scientific evidence confirming that the way people think and perceive things produces chemicals in the brain that promote either illness or health. In fact, a branch of science is now being devoted to the study of the body/mind connection. It is called Psychoneuroimmunology (si'-ko-noor'-o-im'-yoon-o'-lo-gy), or PNI. PNI begins from the notion that what we think about and perceive in our minds creates chemicals that will support these perceptions. For example, if we are stressed, our bodies take this as a signal to release certain chemicals that will work against us. Imagine ocean waves crashing against rocks on the shore. As the surf continues to do this over a long period of time, the rock will corrode. In much the same way, tension works on our bodies. Without a release from stress, our body and mind will deteriorate. This chapter is based upon these scientific findings.

Self-help techniques offer ways for an individual to trigger the chemicals in the brain that foster health. These are not a substitute for problems that call for professional counseling, but they can help. Someone with chronic or major depression may need medication, and only a doctor can decide this. Once a total care program is established, the individual can proceed with a self-help regime.

USING IMAGERY

A simple experiment will demonstrate how you can affect your body's physical changes in much the same way Marge's reactions did. Close your eyes and imagine a tart lemon. See it as clearly and with as many details as you can. It doesn't have to be an actual picture. A sense of it or simply thinking about it will produce the same results. Think of it as being big and juicy. Then imagine you take a big bite into it. Most people will notice the sides of the mouth pucker or begin to water. The lemon was only imaginary, but you fooled your body into responding as if it were real. It created saliva in your mouth. If a lemon is difficult for you to imagine, try anything else you like to eat and see if you can't make your mouth water.

MENTAL PICTURES

Next, try imagining an event that brings back happy memories. Recall a time when you felt peaceful or content, or experienced joy. Allow yourself to get involved in the fantasy. Add as many details to the scene as you can. If you were with a friend, recall what the friend was doing and saying. Where did the scene take place? Was it on the beach or in your room? What can you see, hear, and feel about the original event? Notice how this vision creates a positive sensation. A smile might come to your face, or your chest may feel lighter as you remember the pleasant experience.

Now recall an unpleasant event. Allow yourself enough time to really feel your physical response to the mental picture. Undoubtedly, you will experience some sort of negative sensation. There might be a heavy feeling in your body and a sadness. Everyone is unique, but all of us will experience positive or negative reactions depending upon the images. Not all people visualize easily. Some of us relate better to words. Words we construct in our minds are called self-talk. This is a form of imagery as useful as picture imagery.

RECREATING MEMORIES

Try the above experiment using positive or negative statements instead of images. Describe both a positive and negative experience. This can be done out loud or quietly to yourself. For example: "I remember the time when I was given the best birthday present. I couldn't believe my eyes when this huge box arrived on my doorstep." Using words in this way helps to recreate the event visually as well as emotionally.

These little demonstrations should give you a sense of your own personal power. Once you have gained confidence in your ability to influence your feelings, you are ready to make dramatic changes in your life. The next step is observing your own mind and its many conflicting thoughts. Some of your thoughts are so deep inside that you may be unaware of them. You think countless thoughts in a split second, and only a very few seep into your consciousness. Therefore, the first step in improving your self-image is to become aware of your thoughts. The next exercise will help do this.

DEVELOPING AWARENESS

For the next week, stop whatever you are doing at certain times during the day to observe your thoughts or mental pictures. You can remind yourself to do this by putting stickers on various places at which you are likely to look. The refrigerator, your watch, or your bathroom mirror are all good places. Notice what you are thinking about. Are you being critical, discounting yourself, or being negative in any way?

Write the statements you notice on a piece of paper. Then use your own creativity to turn self-defeating statements into more encouraging ones. The following list of statements are examples of both negative and positive self-talk:

NEGATIVE
- There's no use in trying.
- I'll never make it to my goal.
- No one would ever want to date me.
- No one really cares. What's the use?
- Why am I the only one who has to...?

POSITIVE

- I'm the only one who can take action on the problem.
- I can do anything if I take one step at a time.
- There's bound to be someone for me. I have a good sense of humor and most people enjoy that aspect of me.
- If I need help with something, or just want some company, I can ask for it.
- When I allow myself to be objective, I realize other people have to deal with these things, too.

VISUALIZATION

Visualizing things as you want them to be is extremely helpful in creating an outcome you want. Try observing an existing negative situation and turn it around to imagine yourself calm and in control.

For example, let's suppose you feel nervous before a date. You see yourself fumbling over your words, not having anything to say, perspiring in discomfort, and just generally looking foolish. The first step is to observe this negative mental picture without judging yourself. In other words, don't put yourself down for seeing yourself in this undesirable way. Simply acknowledge the negativity and accept it as something that is true now but needn't be. Then proceed to create an image as you would prefer to see yourself. This is called end-result imagery.

You might see yourself in a relaxed posture and talking easily; however, don't fall into the pitfall of perfection. It's okay if you're not perfectly relaxed and in charge. One image that can prove helpful is seeing yourself with a mild degree of discomfort, accepting it as human nature. Perhaps your slight imperfections lead you and your date to some laughter as you each poke fun of your shortcomings. Now you can envision yourself having a great time with things in a less than ideal state.

PHYSICAL ACTIVITY OR PLAY

One of the laws of physics states that no two masses can occupy the same space at the same time. In other words, a desk and a chair cannot be in the same place at the same time. In much the same way, negative emotions cannot coexist with motion. That dismal feeling seemingly fills space within the body. When there is motion—physical exercise, or any type of play involving moving the arms, legs, and body around—depression or negativity disappears. In this way, a sufferer can exert some amount of control over depression. The obstacle, however, is in the nature of depression. There is often a heavy, lethargic feeling

Physical activity definitely does more than keep your body healthy—it can keep your mind healthy as well, and help you keep setbacks in a proper perspective.

and a desire to wallow in it. It takes a great deal of motivation to overcome this natural tendency. This is not to say a person suffering from chronic or major depression can be cured by exercising. It simply means body movement will assist in lifting the spirits, and the mood change will last longer than the period of activity. The chemicals released in the brain during movement remain for a period of time. If exercise is done on a regular basis, the entire body chemistry will alter and give long-term rewards.

There is an additional advantage. When the sufferer's mood is lifted, he or she is more inclined to act in positive ways. With success comes more success. When acting in more positive ways, an individual is encouraged. Feelings of encouragement prompt him or her to continue the process. Instead of a vicious negative cycle, a positive one begins. The momentum of the entire process can pull someone out of gloom and into a more confident way of life.

NUTRITION

Dee's parents were recently divorced. Not surprisingly, this depressed her and she began to have trouble concentrating in school. After a year of adjustment to her new situation, she thought the problem would go away. When depression continued to disrupt her life despite how well she thought she was coping, she consulted a therapist who took a holistic approach. Holistic means treating the body and mind together.

The therapist discovered a change in Dee's eating habits. At about the same time her parents split up, she began to lose interest in food. She'd grab a bite while on the run, never giving a thought to its nutritional value. Some days, she wouldn't eat at all. Other days, her diet consisted of a doughnut for breakfast and a can of soup for dinner. This pattern continued even after she settled into her new life living with her mom.

Her doctor told Dee about the role food plays in emotional stability. She learned the importance of feeding her brain as well as her body. She found out how the blood carries food, such as digested proteins, carbohydrates, fats, and other nutrients to all the organs in her body. The cells in her body burn nutrients with oxygen to derive usable energy and maintain life. Her reduction in strength over the past year was no longer a mystery. She had failed to supply the cells with the necessary nutrients with which to obtain energy. Armed with this information, she proceeded to change her ways to include plenty of good nutritious food. In a few weeks, she was back to her normal self.

A BALANCED LIFESTYLE APPROACH TO EMOTIONAL HEALTH

Mental health requires a balance of many aspects in life. The following chart shows seven essential ingredients that go into a successful life.

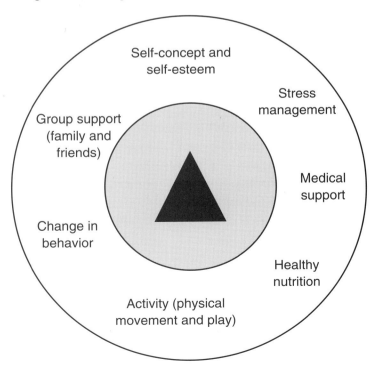

Listening to relaxation tapes can help you reduce stress and feel healthier.

A sense of well-being can only exist when all the body's needs are satisfied. Hippocrates of ancient Greece was the first physician who recognized a connection between food and how people feel. Since then, science has proven his observation. One experiment showed an increase in the ability to tolerate pain when subjects ate foods containing certain substances. In another study, people who ate a high-carbohydrate, low-protein diet showed a significant decrease in their ability to concentrate. These foods also affected their ability to think clearly.

Further information shows a direct relationship between illnesses such as bipolar disorder and depression and cravings for carbohydrates, such as sugar and starchy foods. Good nutrition is not the answer to all emotional disorders, but it can help people improve their mental outlooks. You can try other changes to improve your mental well-being:

Behavior change. Striving for small changes in behavior can go a long way toward success in modifying one's overall negative attitude. Perhaps your difficulty is in talking with members of the opposite sex. Make a plan for a slight behavior adjustment. Set a goal to smile at a boy or girl sitting at the next table in the cafeteria. After you've done that for a week, set the next goal to include saying hello. A balanced lifestyle approach to emotional health means accepting small changes to build bigger ones.

Group support. Elicit the help of friends and family members. Express your need for encouragement, praise, and support. Tell them you are making an effort to change your actions, thoughts, and feelings. Your ability to become more positive and get through difficult times can be strengthened by support from parents and friends. They can offer new perspectives that help your self-esteem.

Stress management. Whether the problem is a major disorder or a less severe problem, a reduction in stress will have a profound effect in helping you successfully overcome a difficulty. Watch some funny movies, read a humorous book, or do other activities that will provide you with an enjoyable release of tension. Regular sessions of self-hypnosis or other relaxation techniques decrease the body's physiological response to strain and anxiety. Take a class in yoga or simply take the time to listen to your favorite music. Nondirected or aimless television watching does not create a relaxation response in your body. Sitting hour after hour spaced out, or flipping from channel to channel is a passive, nonproductive way of eliminating stress. A deliberate choice to watch a particular show for a half-hour or hour, however, will serve to rest and rejuvenate your mind and body.

Medical support. When the situation calls for it, get a physical check-up. Just like Dee's nutrition problem, some things, such as depression, are made worse by how you treat your body. Be sure to call upon those professionals who can guide you to a healthy recovery.

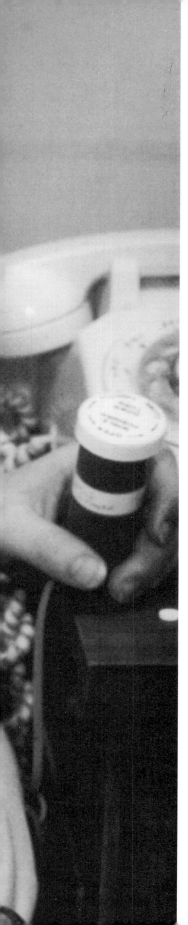

5

DEALING WITH SUICIDE

It is characteristic of wisdom not to do desperate things.
—Henry David Thoreau

James was a very sensitive person. He picked up on people's moods very easily. This was particularly true when it came to his parents' frame of mind. Mr. and Mrs. Devon each had their own beliefs about how children should be raised. Mr. Devon expected youngsters to learn discipline and self-control. Mrs. Devon felt youth was a time for exploration and learning through trial and error. She also believed fun and enjoyment were part of growing up healthy. Each felt the other had the more extreme point of view. When James' mother allowed certain freedoms, his father would become resentful about her lax attitude. The reverse would create conflict between them, too. When Mr. Devon enforced certain rules, Mrs. Devon would react with negative feelings toward her husband.

All of this family conflict created confusion in James. He naturally wanted peace between his parents, but didn't know how to bring it about. His sensitivity made him that much more susceptible to the unhappiness in his home. Someone else might not have taken his parents' problems so seriously. Another person might have ignored all this fussy attention and focused on improving his or her own life and left the parents to take care of themselves.

One day, James came home from school and noticed his mother quietly drinking coffee at the

In the past few decades, the rate of teenage suicide has risen steadily. People who are under such severe emotional distress that they talk about taking their own life are crying out for help.

kitchen table. His dad was looking out the window in a blank stare. There was no obvious sign of an argument, yet James could tell they were in the midst of one. This made it even more confusing for him. He knew he was feeling something, but he wasn't sure what it was. The kind of fights his parents had were usually very subtle and indirect. He felt he couldn't say anything, because, on the surface, nothing was really going on. If he asked either one of them about what he sensed, he was met with denial. "Oh, I'm just a little under the weather," his mom would say. His dad wouldn't even admit there were any emotions at all: "Well son, I'm just trying to decide how to dig up that old dead tree out there in the yard."

HELPLESSNESS

James felt helpless and hopeless over this situation. He believed his parents' disagreements stemmed from him. "I'm sure if I weren't here, they wouldn't be having these problems," he thought. He also experienced a great deal of inner conflict for which he had no solution. Because he grew up surrounded by emotional denial, he lacked the tools to decipher his feelings. He was having difficulty living with his inner turmoil. His inner thoughts might have sounded like this: "I'm trying to cope, but I can't deal with this pain anymore." He made a decision to kill himself.

Many myths and misconceptions exist about the motives of those who kill themselves. When a person is suicidal, sometimes loved ones misinterpret the danger: "Oh, he's just spoiled. When he doesn't get what he wants, he acts out." This is a common belief among people who don't understand the deep despair it takes to end one's life. Emotional needs are as basic to mental health as food, clothing, and shelter are to physical health. When the requirement for emotional nourishment is not fulfilled, feelings of total hopelessness and helplessness set in.

James was fortunate. His parents were home when he tried to hang himself. They found him before it was too late. They suddenly realized that professional help was needed. Several sessions with a therapist revealed how James' family functioned—or, more accurately, didn't function. James' own temperament played an important role in his problem. His parents had difficulties of their own, but were using the issue with James to avoid looking at themselves and their own discontent with each other. Once the specialist pointed these things out, the family was able to air their feelings. Mr. and Mrs. Devon began talking more about themselves. This allowed James to let go of some of his concern for them and deal with his own problems instead.

James' serious nature made him overly sensitive to others. This caused him a great deal of pain. On one level, his motive for suicide was to find a way out of a situation he could no longer tolerate. Suicide was the only option he knew of to end his misery. There was also the issue of attention. While his parents were spending a great deal of time thinking about what was good for James, there was no actual attention being paid to James himself. All of their time and energy were devoted to talking about him, not with him. When James decided to kill himself, he chose a time when his parents were home. He subconsciously knew he would be discovered. This was not a spoiled, "look at me" attempt at attention, however. James' need is better expressed as, "Look at me, help me! I can't live with this pain anymore!"

GRIEF AND JEALOUSY

B onita was a typical teen in many ways. She was wrapped up in socializing, such as making the cheerleading squad. She did well enough in school to get by. Her boyfriend was on the football team. This boosted Bonita's popularity as well. His friendship meant a great deal to her and she frequently imagined their future together. One Saturday night at a party, everything seemed terrific. She had a few drinks and was just beginning to feel a little lightheaded. She was standing with several of her friends sharing some laughs when out of the corner of her eye, she noticed her boyfriend with his arms around her best friend. They were kissing passionately for what seemed like an hour. Not believing what she saw, she stepped a little closer toward the couple. When the two spotted her, they stopped their embrace and proceeded to deny what was going on. "It's not what you think," said Michael.

So much anger swelled in Bonita that she didn't even hear the rest of his explanation. Instead, she walked out of the party, got in her car, and went home. The whole drive was spent thinking of some way to get back at them. She felt hurt and betrayed, but all she was able to focus on was her anger. Anger was a safe emotion for her. Feeling vulnerable made her too uncomfortable. "I know what I'll do," she thought. "I'll take a bunch of pills. When I'm dead, they'll feel bad they were the cause of this." When she arrived home, she found her mother's sleeping pills. After taking a handful, she realized what she'd done. She knew she really didn't want to die. She tried desperately to get some help, but the pills had already begun to take effect. Bonita was clutching the telephone when the paramedics found her. She didn't know that the alcohol in her system compounded the effects of the medicine she swallowed; it was as if she'd taken twice as many pills.

Bonita is only a fictional person, but a growing number of teenagers attempt suicide in just this way out of need for attention. Their deaths are very real. The motives of young people who attempt suicide vary. All, however, are a mixture of emotions. These emotions are a pull between loving and hating;

between feeling a desperate hopelessness and wanting a solution to problems at the very last minute; between wanting to communicate with friends and family and wanting to break away from them. Bonita wanted Michael to know her feelings of hurt and anger, yet running from him was what she did. It was a deadly mistake.

A combination of drives is always at work when a person attempts suicide. Bonita attempted to manipulate the feelings of her boyfriend and her best friend. In her hysteria, she never stopped to consider that she wouldn't be alive to get satisfaction from their suffering. Her effort to manipulate others was a desperate act to try to take control of her own life.

A sense of loss and rejection often provokes a teen to end his or her life. Bonita felt this way when Michael showed his affection for another girl. Her feelings of rejection were compounded by the loss of what she believed to be a secure future with him and her trust in her friend. This caused more stress than she could handle.

SUICIDAL EXCUSES

S uicide among teens has been on the rise in the United States for decades. Back in 1955, the number of suicides per 100,000 people between the ages of 15 and 24 was 4.1. This figure rose to 6.2 ten years later. In the seventies, it had jumped to an astounding 11.8 suicides per 100,000. In the 1990s, the teenage suicide rate has leveled off somewhat at 11.3. This is still an alarming and regrettable statistic.

What are the reasons given for a suicide? Suicide is a three-fold problem: psychological, sociological, and biological. To believe suicide stems from only one category often falls short of the real answer. Consider this: Studies show a higher incidence of suicide among twins. The suicides were all committed by identical twins, not fraternal twins. Another study shows a higher rate of suicides in biological relatives as opposed to adopted relatives. This information might support the existence of a genetic factor that may be partially responsible for the problem. Other research has revealed a difference in the brain chemistry of many people who have committed suicide. A chemical that appears lower in those who suffer from a form of depression has been found to be consistently lower in two-thirds of those who either committed suicide or attempted it.

Experts warn against blaming a biological factor as the sole source of suicidal impulses. Biological elements alone probably can't trigger suicidal behavior. They can only make some people more susceptible to impulsive, aggressive, and potentially suicidal behavior. A person with this same biological make-up, but raised in a loving, nurturing environment may never experience a

Loneliness, rejection, pressures at school or at home—all these can be contributing factors to teen suicide.

suicidal urge. Sociological studies offer a different perspective. Two sociologists studied changes in suicide rates. They suggest a direct relationship between involvement with others and the level of risk for being suicidal.

THE WARNING SIGNS

The clues present in someone headed for suicide are actually the same as those that define depression. Since depression precedes the attempt, it is best to learn to recognize the signs of depression. A combination of indicators can determine if a person is suicidal or not. Since we all feel depressed at times, it is necessary to look at a total picture before becoming concerned. There are other reasons teens may exhibit warning signs of depression or suicide, yet not actually suffer from the problem. For example, their need to become independent from the family may prompt them to spend more time in their own room. This may not necessarily mean they are withdrawing from friends or family.

Sometimes, there aren't any obvious signs at all. This is true for a small percentage of teens who attempt suicide. Those who are used to hiding pain even from themselves might take their own life without revealing any clues beforehand. Take the case of the overachiever. She never wanted to let anyone down. She participated in normal teenage activities until the day before she died. A friend described her as excited about starting her senior year, but she was clearly determined to end her life. Fortunately, most people who attempt suicide reveal some distinctive signals. Friends and family who educate themselves about these have a good chance of helping the sufferer. Here are some warning signs to look for:

Sudden or dramatic changes in behavior. Jeannie, who was normally a quiet and shy person, began to act out. She'd been afraid to date and even cringed when boys said hello to her in the hallway at school. Suddenly, she had a string of boyfriends. Even boys from the school across town began asking her out. Her mother noticed the extreme change in her and probed for a reason. After a great deal of reluctance, Jeannie revealed an upsetting secret. Her friend's father had recently molested her. The shock threw her into a depression. Her acting out and sleeping with anyone and everyone was her way of attempting to deal with her feelings.

Any dramatic change in behavior, whether it is a change from being outgoing to quiet and moody or just the opposite, is reason to suspect a severe disturbance has occurred. It is important to recall the basic personality of the individual and compare it to the current behavior. An extreme change should be regarded as a warning.

Feelings of self-hatred and worthlessness. "I wish I were pretty. It's too bad I'm stuck with such an awfully big nose." "I struck out and the bases were loaded. I should be kicked off the team." "I'll never learn this dance routine. I might as well not even try."

These are all statements made by people who feel worthless. Their self-hatred is evidenced in their thinking patterns. They are very critical of themselves. The positive is ignored and they focus only on the negative. The hatred is a reflection of their deep emotional pain. People hurting this much are susceptible to wanting to end their lives.

Sleeping problems. Difficulty in sleeping may be another symptom of depression. People might toss and turn for hours and finally fall asleep at 4:00 in the morning. When teens suffer from this, they often sleep later into the day. Some people misinterpret this as laziness. In truth, they require the rest, but are unable to get it in a normal way.

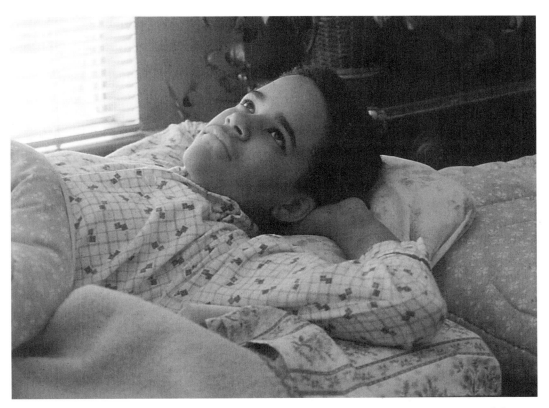

A chronic sleeping problem, sleeping too much or not enough, is one symptom of deeper emotional conflicts that can lead to suicide.

Another pattern of sleep disturbance is waking up several times during the night. With this type of problem, the individual may fall asleep easily enough, but only sleep for a couple of hours at a time.

The reverse can be a signal of a problem, too. Sleeping more than a normal amount can be an attempt to avoid things. Tara was one such case. She slept 16 to 18 hours a day. She later took an overdose of pills and ended up in the hospital. When the sleep could no longer provide an escape for her pain, she resorted to more determined means to block out the hurt—she took sleeping pills.

Fatigue. Sometimes, depression is disguised as physical exhaustion. People with this symptom will wake up tired, as if they hadn't slept at all. They may have a lethargic look. It's as if a 100-pound weight is strapped to their backs. In fact, the unresolved emotions create a true physical burden. A cocked, downward turn of the head and eyes that seem to hug the ground may be visible signs of this internal feeling.

Lack of interest in friends. "I just walked around wanting to be alone. I didn't have any friends. No one wanted to be around me," said Seth. Seth not only wanted to be alone, but created a self-fulfilling prophecy: Others didn't want to be around him. Suicidal people withdraw from everyone. Seth's self-esteem was so bad that pulling away served as a protective wall, sealing in the hurt.

Poor performance at school or work. A change in any area in which a person was once functional shows a deterioration in the state of mind. The person must expend a great deal of effort to perform at work or at school. Effort takes energy, and energy is severely lacking in one who is suicidal.

Dramatic change in appetite. Eating interests, like sleeping patterns, are either overindulged or lacking when someone suffers from suicidal tendencies. A teenage boy with a normally hearty appetite may go for long periods without eating. A girl who is obsessed with her looks may lose interest in her appearance and go on eating binges.

Irritability and restless behavior. A person in this state of mind is sometimes described as "touchy." For example, Gene loses his temper for no apparent reason and expresses anger easily. His rage prompts such an upheaval that people are actually afraid to approach him. "Just forget it and leave me alone," he barks when his girlfriend asks if he wants to go get a bite to eat. In an effort to protect himself from further hurt, he uses anger to keep people at a distance.

Some people even develop a sensitivity to sounds. David's irritability was so severe that everyday sounds of the school bell, classroom doors closing, horns honking, even the telephone ringing at home, made him want to hold his ears in pain.

Taking unusual risks. It is not unusual for a teen who has been depressed to get in a car and take his aggressions out by using a heavy foot on the gas pedal. The feeling of speeding and driving recklessly acts as a vent for pent-up anger, resentment, and frustration. Doing this to show off is distinctly different from acting out of a disturbed emotional state. When a reckless act is done during a depressed or suicidal frame of mind, the teenager will show little concern for what may result.

Thinking or talking about death. Talking about death should always be taken as a sign the individual is troubled. Sally was met with a light-hearted response to her preoccupation with death and dying. "If you'd spend the same energy on your school work as you do on wondering what it's like to be dead, you'd probably get 'A's," her father told her. Later, she cut her wrists to prove she was earnest.

Giving away possessions. When someone offers her favorite things, such as clothing, a stereo, jewelry, or virtually anything she considers important, it's best to question her motives:

"Why are you giving me all these things?" asked Mary.

"I just won't be needing them anymore," Judy replied in a monotone. Judy was often generous with her things. She enjoyed sharing her joys with others, but Mary had heard Judy talking about death during the last several weeks. She also recognized several other symptoms that led her to believe Judy was getting ready to take her life. This immediately alerted Mary to take action and find some help for her friend.

HELPING SOMEONE WHO IS SUICIDAL

A person on the verge of suicide feels like no one understands him or his problems. Allowing him to talk and express his feelings is the first step toward breaking through the barrier of isolation. Empathy is an important element in this process. This is the ability to express compassion for the problem without judging the person or feeling sorrow or pity for them. "Active listening" is a technique for reassuring the talker that he is being understood. Paraphrasing his statements and offering them as feedback makes him feel his message is being received. Martha studied this technique in a class designed to train peer counselors. She learned to role play with other classmates. Here's an example:

Dennis: "I hate my parents. They are always grounding me. If I do the slightest thing different from the way they want me to, they tell me I'm being defiant."

Martha: "So what you're saying is that when you do things in a different way than your parents want you to do, they punish you. This causes you to hate them."

Dennis: "Yes, that's right. When my father tells me it's his house and I have to do things his way, I want to move out and show him I can do what I want in my own house."

Martha: "What you're telling me is that you want to get your own house so you can prove to your father that you can do things your own way."

Dennis: "I guess if I had my own house, I would want people to do things the way I wanted. I mean, I wouldn't want someone coming in and doing what they wanted to do in my house. I guess that's a lot like my father's point of view, isn't it?"

Dennis appreciated that Martha understood his feelings. It may not have changed how his parents behaved toward him, but it altered his own feelings about their behavior. Displaying empathy to another is one healing technique.

If you suspect someone is suicidal, go to someone you trust or convince your friend or family member to seek out help. Taking on the responsibility alone is not advisable. Community resources exist to direct you to the help you need. Police officers, firefighters, and religious leaders have chosen these fields in part because they want to help. Emergency programs exist in every community, too. Suicide prevention hotlines can be found in the phone book along with the YMCA, YWCA, and substance abuse prevention programs. A call to a hospital emergency room, 911, the local police, or a fire dispatch number are all excellent ways to get immediate assistance.

If someone you know is contemplating suicide, don't wait—call a suicide hotline or other crisis intervention service. You will find them listed in your local phone book. If you can't find one, talk to an adult you trust, and ask them for help.

WHAT IF YOU FEEL SUICIDAL?

S ome studies reveal that between 35 and 90 percent of all young people seriously consider taking their lives at some point during their teen years. This fact alone can help you make a decision to get help. You are not alone. Others have felt this way and have had the courage to confront the pain, deal with it, and recover.

Don't wait for a crisis. The beginning stages of a depression should alert you to seek out help. The nature of depression is to pull you deeper and deeper in until you no longer have any motivation whatsoever to reach out. This emotional state is like quicksand that can come rapidly and unexpectedly. If you have any suicidal thoughts, find some help.

Create a support list. This is a group of names of people you can call at any time. Compile this list when you are feeling relatively okay. Then, in a moment of desperation, when you won't have the ability to think about who to call, those names will be readily available. Having this list of people in hand may help you get past the urge to withdraw entirely. This list should include relatives, friends, or family friends; a school counselor, teacher, or administrator; the police or fire departments; counselors from your church; psychologists, or psychiatrists; emergency programs such as hotlines and teen talk lines. Be sure to update the list if you move or change schools.

6

GETTING HELP

Although the world is full of suffering,
it is also full of the overcoming of it.
—Helen Keller

By the time Joseph was 13 years old, he was uncontrollable. Fights with his stepfather were so loud that concerned neighbors called the police on several occasions. He responded to curfews and restrictions with rage. These confrontations always ended with physical outbursts, such as smashing dishes; then Joseph would disappear. He was caught stealing from a local store. His negative behavior escalated uncontrollably until one day his father found him drinking. Joseph's parents had reached their limit and finally decided professional help was necessary.

They didn't want to put Joseph in a hospital, but they knew they could no longer handle him at home. In talking to their minister, they discovered the existence of residential treatment centers. Joseph and his family talked over the problem with a social worker. They all decided placement in an appropriate facility, where he could receive the help he needed, would be best. They placed him in a group home, where he learned to deal with authority in a more positive way. He attended weekly group sessions with other residents and private therapy sessions with a counselor. His family also attended group meetings at the center, during which they learned better ways to interact with Joseph. After three

Sometimes only professional help will aid a young person's recovery from an emotional crisis. Don't ignore drastic changes in behavior, and if you or someone you know is hurting, get help.

months, he was able to go home on weekends once a month. His behavior improved tremendously. After living at the treatment center for a year, he returned home.

Remember anorexic Susan from Chapter 2? Her eating disorder progressed to a dangerous point. The therapist to whom she was referred recognized the urgency of her situation. Her parents were advised to hospitalize her immediately. She needed constant monitoring and intense psychological care. Susan's parents found a hospital program for eating disorders and had her admitted. After six weeks, she had enough recovery and lost some of her fear of eating. She began to gain some of her weight back and was able to return home. Her continued program of recovery included several visits a week to Overeaters Anonymous and private sessions with her therapist. The OA program taught her the importance of talking about her problems. "Our disease is one of isolation," explained her sponsor. She began to reach out to people in ways she never tried before.

SELF-HELP

Numerous resources are available to help those with emotional problems. Self-help groups can offer assistance in ways professionals can't and vice versa. The most well-known self-help groups are those commonly referred to as "12-step" programs. "Twelve-step" program is a term used to refer to groups that use the twelve steps of Alcoholics Anonymous (AA). These groups consist of people with a similar problem gathering together to share in their battles for recovery. For example, people with a drinking problem attend AA and people with a drug problem attend Narcotics Anonymous (NA). Those who attend are at different stages of their rehabilitation.

Meeting with peers to achieve emotional recovery has many advantages. People with problems often believe others don't know how they feel. They assume they are the only ones who suffer in this way, but, in fact, this attitude plays a major role in creating the problem in the first place. Seeing others with the same complex problems helps participants overcome feelings of isolation. Nothing succeeds like success; alcoholics at the depths of their illnesses can watch others recuperate from their own versions of the same inferno and be filled with hope. "If they can do it, so can I," echoes in their minds.

A third asset to peer recovery is summed up in the word synergism. This means the whole is bigger and more powerful than the sum of its parts. The group as a whole can do what the individual alone can't. A final advantage has to do with authority. A person feeling bad about him- or herself may rebel against someone with professional status. He or she may feel the professional has only book knowledge of the problem. In a 12-step group, all the participants

Meeting with others your age to share experiences will help you realize that you are not the only one with an emotional problem.

know about the problem from first-hand experience. They have experienced the depths of the problem in their own lives. As a result, they may have more respect for what they learn from other participants.

On the other hand, a professional can offer expertise in areas that are also needed to heal an emotional disorder. No one can stop alcoholics from drinking, for instance. This is something they need to do for themselves; however, the reasons they began to drink must be addressed. A professional can offer therapy to help them overcome some of these tensions. Usually, the best results are achieved when both peer group and professional counseling are used; one complements the other.

Among the best-known groups who have adapted the philosophy of AA are Narcotics Anonymous, Gamblers Anonymous, Overeaters Anonymous, Parents Anonymous (a child abuse prevention program), Emotions Anonymous, Smokers Anonymous, Co-dependents Anonymous or CODA (a group for those with dysfunctional relationships), Al-Anon (a support for friends and family of alcoholics), and Alateen (an Al-Anon program for teens). Each of these groups is founded on the belief that compulsion is incurable; however, their work can drive the destructive behavior into remission (that is, make it stop) for long periods of time. If people with these diseases faithfully practice the 12 steps of their particular program one day at a time, they can be free from the effects of their compulsions.

The 12-step philosophy labels the illness a progressive one; that is, if the addict continues to practice his drug of choice—whether it is food, narcotics, alcohol, gambling, or any other compulsion—it will get worse. By the same token, the disease will continue to worsen if the sufferer slips back into compulsive actions after a period of abstinence.

Each of these 12-step programs recommends refraining from the behavior entirely. Abstaining from drugs and alcohol are self-explanatory. Probably the most difficult to understand is how to avoid the compulsion for food, as eating is necessary for survival. People cannot eliminate it from their lives as they can other substances.

Overeaters Anonymous supports a program of planned, moderate meals. The compulsion occurs when choices are made during moments of stress. In fact, it appears at unpredictable times without rhyme or reason. Therefore, the preplanning of meals only helps to reduce the inclination to take that first compulsive bite. Assistance for this, as in all 12-step programs, is provided by a sponsor. A sponsor is someone in the program who already has some degree of recovery. He or she shows a new member how to work the twelve steps.

Members of Overeaters Anonymous are not all overweight. Bulimics and anorexics share the same compulsion for food. It just doesn't manifest in the same way physically. Each has found recovery in the OA program, but it takes courage and the support of others who understand the struggle to maintain a healthy weight.

TREATING THE ENABLER

The focus of Al-Anon and Alateen is on the friends or family members of an alcoholic or addict. Participants are taught about the disease. They are shown how they may be contributing to the pattern that keeps the alcoholic sick. Ways of detaching from this routine are described. The friend or family member can truly help the addict's recovery by not enabling him or her.

Enabling an alcoholic occurs when someone excuses the behavior. Parents might ignore their child's continuous absences from school, which they know are a result of drinking. Bailing a child out when he or she gets arrested is another means for hiding and excusing actions. On the other hand, some teens may be put in the awkward position of calling their parents' bosses to say the parents are sick, when, in fact, hangovers prevent them from showing up at work. All of this protects addicts from the consequences of their actions. If the children act as enablers, the parents have no motivation to stop drinking because they are shielded from any potentially painful results. Participants in programs like Al-Anon learn how to break this behavior pattern.

When one individual family member abuses drugs or alcohol, other family members (usually a spouse or older child) often act as enablers—helping the abuser to function and thus keep the addiction going, instead of helping him or her break the habit.

HOW EMOTIONAL HEALTH IS GAUGED

Are you emotionally stable? Do you think you might need professional help? Emotional health varies from time to time in every individual. People with stable states of emotions will stay within certain guidelines. Others have drastic mood swings.

Dr. Hans Selye described the stages we go through in response to stress. They are alarm, adaptation, and exhaustion. During the first stage, we are able to confront something threatening our existence by releasing hormones that give us the strength and energy to combat the threat. During the second stage, adaptation sets in. Different hormones kick in and allow us to keep ourselves on an even keel. We react to the stress, control ourselves appropriately, and maintain stability for as long as the stress continues.

What happens when the stress overwhelms our bodies and persists too long? Or when the stress is increased? That's when the third stage begins: exhaustion. This is the stage when one's threshold for pain (emotional, physical, or environmental) decreases. Our resistance to illness is lower, and we become unable to adapt. We then become susceptible to more serious emotional disorders.

There are five stages of emotional health:

1. *Normal adaptability.* This is our ability to cope with changes in circumstance while maintaining a fair amount of motivation to continue with life's daily tasks.

2. *Emergency behavior.* This is our ability to respond to emergency or high stress situations appropriately and then return to normal adaptability when the crises are over. Examples of emergency situations might be a school exam, a deadline for homework, the break-up or loss of an important relationship (such as a boyfriend or girlfriend), the loss or impairment of health, etc.

3. *Neurotic coping styles.* In this stage, the individual reacts to an emergency situation where none exists. A phobia is a good example of this. No actual danger exists when an agoraphobic panics while waiting in line at the supermarket, yet he or she responds as if there is an emergency.

4. *Neurotic personality.* Here, the neurotic ways of coping become fixed parts of the individual's make-up. Even if someone treats him or her in a positive way, the neurotic personality exhibits disruptive or destructive behavior. He or she becomes defensive and is unable to make use of situations in a positive way for personal growth.

5. *Psychotic behavior and conduct disorders.* Disruptive patterns of behavior are present in all phases of one's daily routine. The individual may not be able to work consistently. He or she may go from job to job or simply be unable to go to work or school at all. There is chronic conflict with family, friends, school, and the law. The individual has needs that can't seem to be fulfilled and is unable to address the needs of others.

OTHER RESOURCES

B ooks and tapes serve as additional resources for self-help. Self-improvement materials constitute a multi-billion dollar industry. The business is as big as it is because of the millions of people who suffer from similar problems. Books are available on techniques to help overcome depression, anxiety, phobias, and just about every other form of emotional disorder.

Writing in a journal can be very therapeutic and healing. In fact, it is a regular part of the 12-step programs. Emotional disturbances can be magnified when feelings are kept inside. Using a journal as an outlet for these emotions not only helps people purge their negative effects, but also helps them sort out their confusion.

PROFESSIONAL HELP

M embers of the clergy are often educated in the fields of therapy and counseling. The combination of their training in therapy and their background in religion offers a well-rounded approach to many problems. The therapy does not necessarily include religious preachings. Some people may prefer it, however, because there is a certain comfort level in knowing the therapist holds similar beliefs. The clergy can also serve as a good lead to other forms of help. They can advise you where to find community and private mental health services, for example.

School guidance counselors are also good resources. They generally don't provide counseling of an emotional nature; but, they can guide teens to other services. Guidance counselors are often called upon to help in crisis situations. For example, a girl who discovers she is pregnant may need to be guided to a woman's clinic. A teen who is upset about a family matter and doesn't know where to turn can certainly go to a school counselor for assistance. If a therapist is needed, the counselor can set up an appointment with the school psychologist. Like most school psychologists, that school psychologist may provide only limited emotional counseling, but if more is appropriate, he or she can recommend a good therapist in the community.

Severe situations may call for hospitalization. The turmoil of everyday life may interfere with one's ability to cope with an emotional difficulty. A hospital can provide a controlled environment. The predictability of the rules and structure allows an adolescent to work out problems in a safe atmosphere. Sometimes, removing the teen from the things that were causing the problem—tensions at school, family stress, hanging around drug users, or conflicted relationships—eases enough of the pressure to let him or her get a better perspective. The decision for hospitalization is partly based on the teen's ability to receive adequate treatment in the community. In some cases, finances will determine whether this is a viable option. If the family has medical insurance that covers hospitalization, this may be the best option. In other cases, if the situation calls for it, there may be state funding to cover the cost.

IN TREATMENT

In a hospital, an evaluation of the emotional problem is done through testing, interviewing, and observation. The staff's doctors, nurses, social workers, mental health assistants, and psychologists watch and listen to the patient's behaviors and interactions. They observe the patient's responses to rules, to conflicts with other patients, and to reprimands and praise given by staff and others. They pay particular attention to those behaviors that caused the patient difficulty prior to entering the hospital; for example, a teen who repeatedly argued with teachers and was verbally aggressive to others does the same in any situation. The hospital setting allows for the staff to observe this behavior and provide treatment while it is occurring.

Daily activities in a hospital may include meals, school, group therapy, individual therapy, classes in social skills, relaxation techniques, and assertiveness training. The schedule keeps patients busy and involved. If a patient's stay is a long one, he or she may be permitted to go home on weekends.

After the patient is discharged, an outpatient program is provided to continue the therapeutic progress. The patient will then live at home and return to normal activities, but attend regular group and private therapy sessions at the hospital or in an outpatient program in the community. Parents and family members may be encouraged to attend family therapy and/or parent groups.

In some states, such as California, residential treatment centers are used when the home and family are inadequate to deal with the youngster's problems. They are sometimes used after acute hospitalization and stabilization, when long-term care is needed. The setting can be campus-like, providing cottages to house the residents. Others are single-family homes in residential neighborhoods. Farms and ranches are less common, but are sometimes used. Each home is usually staffed by one or several houseparents. A houseparent acts as a substitute parent. The houseparent reinforces house rules, and offers support and almost anything an actual parent might provide. Residents go to school either on site or at regular public schools in the community. The environment is designed to encourage emotional growth. The idea behind the group home is to recreate a real-life situation in a safe and secure therapeutic environment in which people trained to handle teen problems are close at hand.

In other states, similar facilities exist under different names. Their environments and programs may vary, but the ultimate purpose is always to enable a teen to return to society.

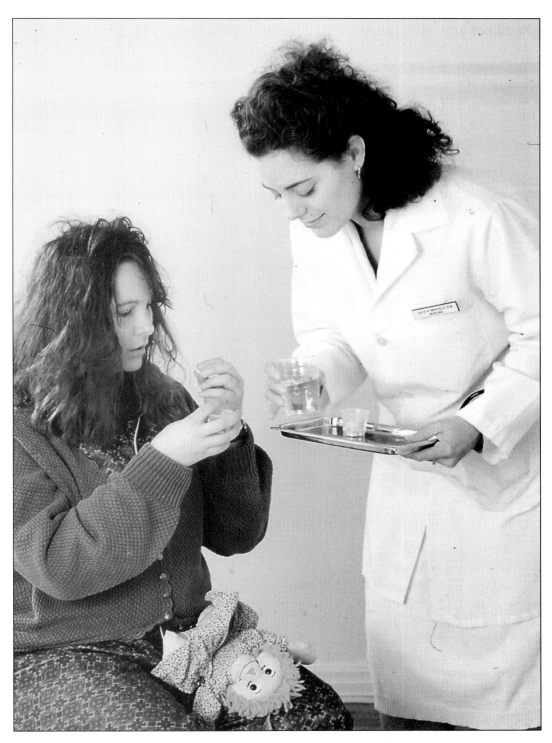

Although many emotional problems can be helped with regular counseling, some cases are so severe that they require hospitalization.

HOW EMOTIONAL HEALTH IS TESTED

The following list describes the tension, mood, relationships, and overall activity level of the five stages of emotional health.

Tension
Stage one: Tension has a cause in the present or the past. You can do something to reduce it.

Stage two: Obvious signs of agitation, sweating, heavy breathing are present. Tension has a cause (exams, recent break-up of a relationship).

Stage three: Signs of tension without obvious reason.

Stage four: Periods of unbearable anxiety without apparent reason.

Stage five: Tension is unbearable without medication. The tension is relieved by psychotic thinking, such as hallucinations.

Mood
Stage one: Changes in mood have an obvious cause. Humor is present even when the mood is intense. Moods pass within a short time.

Stage two: The person is easily upset and moody.

Stage three: Moods last beyond recovery time, as with depression. The person experiences denial of problems, hostility, mild chronic fears and phobias, and blocked emotions, such as love or hate.

Stage four: Moods affect work or play. The person experiences chronic depression or unhappiness. Support from others doesn't help.

Stage five: The person experiences manic behavior and/or feelings unrelated to reality. For example, he or she may feel or act happy at a funeral.

Relationships
Stage one: The person is a friend and has friends. Withdrawal or aggression have obvious causes and pass in a short period of time.

Stage two: The person has anxiety about pleasing others. He or she is overly emotional in relationships and is sometimes irritable.

Stage three: The person demands others to do what he or she wants. He or she holds grudges and feels alienated from others.

Stage four: The person is extremely dependent or manipulative of others.

Stage five: The person has a total inability to relate to others.

Activities
Stage one: The person has enthusiasm and interest in participating in various activities, such as school, hobbies, etc. He or she bounces back from failure, tries again, and continues with interest.

Stage two: The person experiences anxiety over new tasks and situations. He or she may feel overloaded at the slightest deviation from his or her normal routine. Activity may be excessive or severely curtailed, as in those with a bipolar disorder.

Stage three: The person is hyperactive to the point of exhaustion. The person cannot work on his or her own motivation, but requires inspiration or constant feedback to work well.

Stage four: The person avoids new activities, because they do not help to reduce stress. The person usually acts alone, and experiences no pleasure or accomplishment from anything.

Stage five: The activity has become routine. Deviating from a set pattern of activity is very difficult. There is an extreme reluctance to engage in new activities, such as parties, vacations, etc. Change causes discomfort. The only security is in doing familiar tasks.

Source: Adapted from William Gladstone's emotional health test.

THE AIM OF THERAPY

The purpose of therapy is to help people regain an acceptable level of social functioning consistent with their capabilities. For example, if someone was able to keep average grades in school and pursue a reasonably active social life before he became ill, the goal of therapy would be to help him return to the same level of activity and involvement. If he was failing classes and losing interest in his friends, the therapy would be designed to help him regain interest in his studies and other activities.

Many variables may have contributed to the deterioration of his ability to live life normally. Communication between the patient and a loved one may be ineffective or nonexistent. Traumas from past experiences may be unresolved. Whatever the cause, the therapist is there to provide objective feedback in a sheltered arena where the patient can learn to solve his own problems.

In Chapter 1, Beth discovered some family dynamics that caused tension. She was able to see how her anger triggered a response in her mother that prompted her mother to become protective of her father. Her need to shield his feelings actually created more stress. In this situation, the aim of the therapy was to show how each person's interaction contributed to overall feelings of negativity in the family. Once these were revealed, the family could make better choices about how they communicated. Insight such as this is often the goal of therapy.

In Chapter 1, Jim didn't understand why he was depressed. His interest in daily activities deteriorated. He was aware of wanting his father's attention and not knowing how to get it. That alone caused some of his depression. What he didn't understand was that his loss of interest in activities occurred because they weren't really his own interests. Jim joined the football team because his father loved it so much, not because he himself thought it was fun. Once he understood this, he was able to improve his choices based on what he wanted for himself.

Group therapy can provide many lessons. A major advantage of talking with several people about problems is that we remind ourselves that we are not alone. We will see others with similar issues, and can then learn how others handle these problems. This gives us the strength to deal with our own difficulties.

In the case of some emotional disorders, it is the aim of therapy to stabilize the condition. Those with bipolar disorders and schizophrenia often need medication. The medicine helps to eliminate or minimize such things as hallucinations and delusions. For those with bipolar disorder, medicine can also balance their wide emotional pendulums. On medication, the highs aren't so manic, and the lows aren't so deep.

Showing a patient how to reduce stress is a major part of any therapy. Whatever the disorder, whether it is an eating problem, alcoholism, post-traumatic stress, a phobia, or something else, minimizing stress will always improve recovery.

RECOVERY

"I thought I'd be feeling great by now," Shannon said to her therapist. "I don't understand why I still feel down sometimes. The anxiety I feel still leaves me wondering about whether this has helped at all."

Therapy—talking with a counselor or a peer group—helps draw out problems, formulate solutions, and get the patient back on track.

"Do you remember when you first came in to see me?" the doctor asked. "Your depression was so bad you couldn't get out of bed to go to school. On the days you managed to get yourself there, you were filled with such anxiety that you had headaches and stomach aches and other physical symptoms."

"How could I forget those awful times?" said Shannon. "I think those days are permanently etched in my brain."

"Well, how are you doing now by comparison?"

"I go to school most of the time, I do better than average in classes I had been failing, and I even have some friends with whom I feel comfortable."

"I'd say that was a dramatic change in your ability to function, wouldn't you?"

"I guess so," said Shannon. "But when will I stop getting depressed all together?"

Shannon is showing some unrealistic expectations about her recovery. She thinks life is supposed to be happy all the time. Her impossible expectations about life got her into trouble in the first place. When she first entered therapy, she had a drinking problem. She drank because she was sad and thought she should always be happy. Setting some more concrete life goals to avoid emotional problems is important for everyone, including Shannon.

Feeling good about yourself most of the time and coping with the occasions when you don't feel so good is normal. Shannon started out feeling so badly, she was ashamed of herself and her problems. She thought if anyone knew who she was and some of the things she had done, they would reject her. Now she has enough confidence to make some friends. She realized she wasn't perfect, but she wasn't so bad, either. She thought enough of herself to trust that others would accept her the way she was. Her behavior prior to getting help showed a person who was very disturbed. She avoided people, situations, and life in general. Her drinking was a weak way to try to help herself, because it only served to destroy her self-esteem. Now when she feels bad, she is able to do something about it. She can talk to a friend, take a walk, distract herself by playing a computer game, or using any number of other healthy outlets. She takes an active role in solving her problems.

"What do you do when you are anxious now?" prompted the therapist.

"It depends. Sometimes I talk to myself. I might tell myself I can do it, or I might remind myself it will be over soon, or I might even be self-indulgent and let myself feel bad until the feeling passes."

"So your ability to cope with your mood swings has improved, too."

"Yes, I think so. I used to feel good one minute and bad the next. I never knew what to expect. I couldn't make any commitments because I couldn't depend upon how I might feel at any given time. Now when I dip into those sad times, it's usually because something has happened. I'm not caught off guard by my moods."

"You have a sense of control over your life now," said her therapist. "That's the key—to be able to make choices about how you want your life to be, and to be in charge of your reactions to situations you can't control."

Happiness in life defies definition. Maybe it is our ability to feel alive, content, and at peace with ourselves, or to be challenged, interested in things, and fulfilled in our relationships. We can set achievable goals and increase the likelihood that we'll be happy. It's the difference between aiming an arrow into the sky or at a bull's eye. The sky may seem more inviting, but how will we know if we hit where we were aiming? The bull's eye focuses our attention toward a goal that is specific, where we can see the results of our efforts. The fight against emotional disorders begins with recognizing our own feelings, understanding our limitations, and not carrying the whole world on our shoulders. We all have the same worries and fears. We all want to be happy. By helping each other, we can minimize the former and boost the latter.

ADDITIONAL RESOURCES

Your local phone book lists organizations that can provide assistance for emotional disorders. The following are heading suggestions to look under:

Alcoholism Information and Treatment
Attorneys, Law Guardians
Child Guidance
Clinics, Mental Health
Crisis Intervention Services
Drug Abuse and Addiction,
    Information, Treatment, and
    Rehabilitation
Educational Consultants
Handicapped Services and
    Organizations
Human Service Organizations
Hypnotherapy
Information and Referral Services

Learning Disability Counseling
Marriage, Family, Child, and
    Individual Counselors
Mental Health Services
Pastoral Counselors
Physicians, Pediatricians (Infant,
    Child, Adolescent)
Physicians, Psychiatry
Pregnancy Counselling
Psychologists
Social Service Organizations
Suicide Prevention Services
Youth Organizations/Centers

The following is a list of national organizations that offer referrals, support, and other resources:

Al-Anon Family Group Headquarters, 1372 Broadway, New York, NY 10018-0862 (212) 302-7240.

Alcoholics Anonymous World Services, P.O. Box 459, Grand Central Station, New York, NY 10163 (212) 870-3400.

American Academy of Child Psychiatry, 3615 Wisconsin Avenue, N.W., Washington, DC 20016 (202) 966-7300.

American Association for Marriage and Family Therapy, 1717 K Street N.W., Suite 404, Washington, DC 20006 (202) 429-1825. A good resource for couples and families in need of psychotherapy.

American Association of Suicidology, 2459 South Ash, Denver, CO 80222 (303) 692-0985. Can provide names of hotlines, local services, and therapists for suicidal relatives.

American Board of Hypnotherapy, 1805 E. Garry Ave #100, Santa Ana, CA 92705 (800) 872-9996. Referrals for therapists using hypnosis.

Incest and Molestation, Parents United National Headquarters, P.O. Box 952 San Jose, California, 95108 (408) 453-7616.

National Association of Anorexia and Associated Disorders, Box 271, Highland Park, IL 60035 (708) 831-3438.

National Council on Alcoholism. There are local chapters nationwide for community education and treatment referrals. Consult your local phone book.

National Council on Child Abuse and Family Violence 1155 Cannecticut Ave., NW, Suite 400, Washington, D.C. 20036 (800) 222-2000.

National Depressive and Manic Depressive Association, Merchandise Mart, Box 3395, Chicago, IL 60654 (312) 642-0049. Source of information and referrals for treatment of mood-related disorders.

National Institute on Drug Abuse, P.O. Box 2305, Rockville, MD 20852 (301) 443-6245.

National Institute of Mental Health (NIMH), 5600 Fishers Lane, Rockville, MD 20857 (301) 443-2403.

Recovery, Inc., 116 South Michigan Ave, Chicago, IL 60603 (312) 337-5661. Self-help organization for those with emotional problems.

Youth Emotions Anonymous, P.O. Box 4245, St Paul, MN 55104 (612) 647-9712. Self-help organization for youths ages 13-19 with emotional problems.

FOR FURTHER READING

Bandler, Richard. *Using Your Brain for a Change.* Moab, UT: Real People Press, 1985.

Filson, Brent. *There's a Monster in Your Closet: Understanding Phobias.* New York, NY: Julian Messner, 1986.

Greenberg, Harvey R., M.D. *Emotional Illness In Your Family: Helping Your Relative, Helping Yourself.* New York, NY: Macmillan, 1989.

Handly, Robert with Pauline Neff. *Anxiety and Panic Attacks: Their Cause and Cure.* New York, NY: Fawcett, 1987.

Krasner, A.M., Dr. *The Wizard Within.* Santa Ana, CA: A.B.H. Press, 1991.

Landau, Elaine. *Why Are They Starving Themselves? Understanding Anorexia Nervosa and Bulimia.* New York, NY: Julian Messner, 1983.

Lee, Essie E. and Richard Wortman, M.D. *Down Is Not Out: Teenagers and Depression.* New York, NY: Julian Messner, 1988.

Miller, Michael. *Dare To Live: A Guide to the Understanding and Prevention of Teenage Suicide and Depression.* Hillsboro, OR: Beyond Words Publishers, 1989.

Myers, Irma and Arthur. *Why You Feel Down and What You Can Do About It.* New York, NY: Julian Messner, 1983.

GLOSSARY

Addict. One who has a substance abuse habit (drugs, alcohol, food) that dominates his or her behavior.

Adrenaline. The chemical secreted from the adrenal gland that gives the body a boost of energy.

Affective. Relating to, arising from, or influencing feelings or emotions (as in affective disorders).

Afflict. To cause permanent suffering or distress.

Agoraphobia. An abnormal fear experienced in public places. A person who suffers from agoraphobia is called an agoraphobic.

Anorexia nervosa. An eating disorder caused by an abnormal fear of gaining weight. A person afflicted with anorexia is called an anorexic.

Anxiety. A painful uneasiness of the mind often marked by physiological signs of sweating, tension, and rapid pulse.

Binge. An unrestrained indulgence, such as consuming a great quantity of food or alcohol at one time.

Bipolar disorder. Alternating periods between feeling extremely happy and extremely depressed; once called manic depression.

Bulimia. An eating disorder characterized by first binging on food and then purging the body by vomiting. A person afflicted with bulimia is called a bulimic.

Compulsion. An irresistible impulse; for example, binging on food is a compulsion.

Delusion. An abnormal emotional state characterized by false beliefs.

Denial. A refusal to admit the truth or reality of a situation. Alcoholics often deny that they have a problem with drinking.

Depression. A chronic state of feeling sad and helpless.

Dysfunctional. Impaired; a dysfunctional family is unable to maintain healthy relationships among its members.

Emotional disorders. An abnormal physical or emotional condition.

Empathy. Being sensitive to someone else's feelings.

Enabler. Someone who allows a loved one to continue with abusive and self-destructive behavior.

Euphoric. A feeling of well-being or elation.

Hallucination. An imaginary vision.

Hypnotherapy. A therapeutic process guided by a counselor who specializes in hypnotism.

Manic. A state of excessive enthusiasm manifested by emotional and physical hyperactivity, disorganized behavior, and an inappropriately elevated mood.

Obsession. A persistent and disturbing preoccupation with an idea or feeling.

Panic. A sudden, overpowering fright.

Panic attack. A sudden intense apprehension, or fear without apparent cause, often accompanied by physical symptoms of discomfort.

Paranoia. An irrational or excessive concern about what other people are doing or saying.

Phobia. An exaggerated and illogical fear of something.

Post Traumatic Stress Disorder (PTSD). A psychological disorder brought on by a traumatic event or series of events.

Psychiatrist. A medical doctor who treats mental, emotional, and behavioral disorders.

Psychologist. A person educated in the science of mind and behavior.

Psychoneuroimmunology (PNI). The branch of science devoted to the study of the mind's effect on the body and vice versa.

Psychotherapy. The treatment of emotional disorders.

Rationalize. To convince one's self that some thought, action, or behavior is reasonable.

Rehabilitate. To restore or bring to a state of health.

Schizophrenia. An illness characterized by a separation between thought and emotion that produces delusions and bizarre behavior.

Self-esteem. Confidence and satisfaction in one's self.

Stress. Tension that affects the body and the mind. Stress can be caused by a number of internal and external pressures, and may be a factor in the promotion of disease.

Subconscious. The area of emotional activity where an individual has little or no conscious perception.

Suicidal. An impulse to end one's life.

Therapy. A treatment designed to bring about healing.

INDEX

A

affective (mood) disorder(s), 10, 11
   see also bipolar disorder, depression
agoraphobia, 17, 19, 20
Al-Anon, 33-34, 79, 80
Alateen, 79, 80
alcoholic, alcoholism
   as a source of stress, 47-48
   caring for, 33-34
   defined, 10, 32, 33
   denial, 32
   recognizing, 34-36
   symptoms, 32-33
Alcoholics Anonymous (AA), 33, 35, 78, 79
anorexia nervosa, 10, 36, 38-40
anxiety
   case study, 55-56
   relieving, 57-63
anxiety disorder(s), 10, 16-17

B

bipolar disorder, 10, 15-16
bulimia, 36, 38-40

C

compulsive eating disorder, 36, 38-40

D

delusions, 27
depression
   causes of
      loneliness, 13
      parental pressure, 11-12
      school, 13
   recognizing, 13-15
   symptoms of, 30
drinking and driving, 31-32, *see also* alcoholic
drug(s)
   and abuse, 29-31
   tolerance, 31
   withdrawal, 31
dysfunctional relationships, 45-47

E

eating disorder(s)
   and body image, 38-39
   defined, 10
   types of, 36
   who is susceptible, 39-41
emotional disorder(s)
   caring for, 50-53, 63, 78-80, 82-89
   causes
      alcoholism, 47-48
      chemical imbalances, 48-49
      heredity, 48-49
      transitional periods, 49-50
   effects of, 9, 43-45
   in treatment for, 83
   and nutrition, 60-63
   recovery, 88-89
   types of, 10
emotions
   negative, 8, 9
   positive, 7-8
enabler, enabling, 80

H

hallucinations, 27
hypnotherapy, 35-36

M

mental health
   defined, 8-9
mood changes, 30

N

Narcotics Anonymous (NA), 78, 79

O

obsession(s)
   defined, 38
   with food, 38
Overeaters Anonymous (OA), 39, 40, 78, 79, 80

P

S

T

V